*P*rayer

and

*P*ersonality

*D*evelopment

Ways of Growth in Prayer
and Personhood

By

Herbert F. Smith, S.J.

Dimension Books • Denville, New Jersey

Imprimi potest:
Rev. James A. Devereux, S.J.
Provincial
Maryland Province

Nihil obstat:
Sidney C. Burgoyne
Censor Librorum

Imprimatur:
Anthony J. Bevilacqua
Archbishop of Philadelphia

Grateful acknowledgement is hereby made to The Liturgical Press for permission to reprint "A Pilgrimage through Prayer," which first appeared in *Sisters Today* 41:6 (Feb., 1970), pp. 317-333; to *Review for Religious* for permission to reprint "A Method for Eliminating Method in Prayer," "The Nature and Value of a Directed Retreat," and "Consciousness Examen," all of which first appeared in its pages; and to Princeton University Press for permission to use the quotes from C.G. Jung, *Psychological Reflections: An Anthology,* ed., Jolanda Jacobi and R.F.C. Hull, Bollingen Series 31, copyright 1953, © 1970, by Princeton Universiy Press.

Copyright © Corporation of Roman Catholic Clergymen
First American Edition 1989 by Dimension Books
ISBN Number: 0-87193-267-9

Dimension Books, Inc.
Denville, New Jersey 07834

Prayer

and

Personality

Development

Books by Herbert F. Smith, S.J.

Living For Resurrection

God Day By Day

The Lord Experience

The Pilgrim Contemplative

How to Get What You Want From God

Hidden Victory (A Historical Novel of Jesus)

Prayer and Personality Development

Contents

Paved Roads and Cross Country Walks
Ready for the Journey
The Prayer of Simplicity
Distractions
The Next Phase
The Prayer of Faith
Acquired Contemplation
Accompanying Troubles
The Prayer of Quiet

Herbert F. Smith, S.J., with V. Michael Vaccaro, M.D.

Psychological Developments Antecedent to Prayer
Growth of Personality in the Stage of Meditation
Personality Development in the Prayer of Affection
Personality Development in the Prayer of Simplicity
Personality Development in the Prayer of Faith
Personality Development in the Prayer of the Cloud
Personality Development in the Prayer of Quiet

Preparation for Prayer
Finding and Facing Self
Making Points
The Praying Itself
Post-Prayer Activity

About the Author

Herbert Francis Smith, S.J., is an internationally published author of religious works, and a preacher and lecturer with extensive experience as a retreat director, conductor of parish programs, and radio show host. He is currently regional and Philadelphia Archdiocesan Director of the Apostleship of Prayer.

Born in Buffalo, NY, he worked in industry and private business before joining the Society of Jesus in 1951. His work of conducting retreats and of preaching, both in the churches and on the air, has carried him throughout the United States. His articles have appeared in *America, Centrum Ignatianum Spiritualitatis, Homilectic and Pastoral Review, Pastoral Life, The Priest, Review for Religious, Sisters Today, Studies in Formative Spirituality,* and many other publications.

The most popular of Fr. Smith's books is *Hidden Victory, A Historical Novel of Christ,* published in Philadelphia (1984), Manila, and Bangalore.

Fr. Smith has hosted "The Spiritual Exercises of the Air," a weekly radio program in greater Philadelphia, from 1976 to 1988. Eight months spent in the Holy Land researching and writing *Hidden Victory* gave him the opportunity to travel its length and breadth. This personal experience of Jesus' homeland has given a flavor of immediacy to his writing and preaching on the Gospels.

A member of the Fellowship of Catholic Scholars, Fr. Smith is listed in Contemporary Authors.

The Contributors

George A. Aschenbrenner, S.J., is Director of Spiritual Formation at the North American College in Rome. His book, *A God For A Dark Journey,* was published by Dimension Books in 1984. A former Master of Novices, he has wide experience in teaching, giving spiritual direction, and conducting retreats, and has published articles on various aspects of the religious life.

V. Michael Vaccaro, M.D., Director of Group Process and Group Psychotherapy at Hahnemann University, is also engaged in a private practice in psychiatry in suburban Philadelphia, where he lives with his wife and daughters.

Preface

Our search in this book is for knowledge of growth in prayer, and growth in personality through prayer, and the means to achieve both. The ways of prayer are endowed with a certain timelessness. That makes it easy to fall into the trap of thinking these means to growth are timeless. We can, therefore, be surprised by all the reconstruction projects set afoot along the roads to prayer by the Second Vatican Council and the ferment that continues to this day.

Vatican II signaled important changes in the ascent to God, changes which have impacted powerfully on prayer in the decades since. The Council advanced the articulation of incarnational spirituality, and brought it to a focus in the *Constitution on the Church in the Modern World*: "The expectation of a new earth (at the *parousia*) must not weaken but rather stimulate our concern for cultivating this one, for here grows the body of a new human family, a body that even now is able to give some kind of foreshadowing of the new age" (c. 3).

The gravity of this call to serve is accentuated by the debt of service owed the Church: "The member who fails to make his proper contribution to the development of the Church must be said to be useful neither to the Church nor to himself" (*Decree on the Apostolate of the Laity*, c. 1). The "service norm" as a measure of the real ascent to God can no longer be brushed aside.

Not only is the accent on service but, to facilitate serving as God intends, each of us is called to be more active in personally discovering the will of God. Each must discern that will in the signs of the times, in the individual, social, cultural and international needs of humanity. As it is written: "They will all be taught by God" (John 6:45).

Because human beings are already living here on earth the beginnings of their eternal vocation, and must be competent for godly service in the world, the Council issued a ringing call to personal growth in every feasible way in accord with one's station in life. We are to develop our skills and talents to fit ourselves for the service that flows from true concern for our neighbors' salvation and well-being. We are, by word and life, to become potent witnesses of our expectation of Christ's return.

This hands us a formidable task in the realm of prayer, which is our concern here. While losing nothing of the rich tradition of prayer bequeathed the Church by those who have gone before us in the Spirit, we must move forward. We have to take many things which were only germinal in the past–or at least not widely disseminated–and raise them to maturity in the whole Church. The doctrine of discernment of spirits is an example of this. Other powerful helps which flourished in past times, such as the directed retreat originated by St. Ignatius of Loyola, need to be disseminated to meet the needs of our times.

Centrally, we are called to grow. How else meet the world on its own sophisticated terms—the world where we are to find and serve Christ in others? "Therefore one must aim at encouraging the human spirit to develop its faculties of wonder, of understanding, of contemplation, of forming personal judgments and cultivating a religious, moral and social sense" (*Constitution on the Church in the Modern World,* #59). And again, "Every effort should be made to provide for those who are capable of it the opportunity to pursue higher studies so that as far as possible they may engage in the functions and service, and to play the role in society, most in keeping with their talents and the skills they acquire" (# 60).

A flood of books has poured out since the Council to deal with the issues it raised, but too little has been written on the power of prayer to mature the human personality. What follows in this book is, in part, an exploration of that power. It is preceded, however, by a lucid exposition of the classical doctrine of growth in interior prayer. Thus we begin by ascending to the high ground explored and appropriated by the saints and scholars of the past. From there we make our way forward and upward.

No one book can cover the whole terrain of prayer. The effort here is to push forward select frontiers of personal prayer as that prayer carries us upward to God, develops our whole personality in the process, and generates the capacity to attune ourselves to the guidance of the Holy Spirit. When we have thus grown in prayer and grown through prayer, we are suited to play our part as Christians in the world to which the Church today addresses itself so passionately.

I am grateful to Dr. V. Michael Vaccaro, M.D., for collaborating with me in the chapter on "Prayer and Personality Development;" to Fr. George A. Aschenbrenner, S.J., for permission to include in this book his excellent "Consciousness Examen;" and to Fr. Francis F. Burch, S.J., for his expert editorial guidance in preparing the manuscript for submission to the publisher.

Herbert F. Smith, S.J.

Philadelphia, PA

Chapter One

A Pilgrimage Through Prayer

Every person serious about God sooner or later is lured by yearning into the journey of prayer. Pilgrims of prayer, like all epic travelers, consign themselves to danger and disaster unless they have a map to guide them. Without one, they can hardly avoid wrong directions, poorly timed stops, and unnecessary backtracking. Their fears will call the foggy mountain crags impassable, and they will turn back just when one last stubborn effort, guided by the savants and the saints who preceded them, would have carried them across the great divide into the land of God which their prayer had promised.

We do not lack fine road maps for the journey of prayer. Too often, however, they are so complicated by details of localized complexities that pilgrims who are lost without the road map are soon lost in it. Before they can be helped by the plans of city streets they must find out what city of prayer they have come upon.

Our preliminary need is a kind of space-eye view of the whole journey of prayer, analogous to the picture of the whole earth which the astronauts snapped from a hundred thousand mile perspective. That is the view I venture to present.

The journey of prayer set down here is inevitably a distortion of the reality of prayer. No analysis of life can be made without falsifying life to a degree, and no description of our prayer life with God can be expected to capture more than a hint of its wonder and passion and volatility and unchartableness. Still, just as there are common blood types, there are certain main arteries on the journey of developing prayer which are trafficked by the majority of pilgrims. They are really the fortunate ones, for they more easily find help. They may be startled to discover here in rudimentary form the secret autobiography of their prayer growth which they never have revealed and only half remember. The less fortunate will recognize a familiar landmark only here or there. They are the people who for years have wandered the hinterlands of prayer, finding little help from anyone. They may find help in the fine little books, *The Prayer of Faith*, by Leonard Boase, S.J. (Our Sunday Visitor, 1975), or *When the Well Runs Dry*, by Thomas Green, S.J. (Ave Maria Press, 1979).

Paved Roads and Cross Country Walks

Before setting out, we fix in our minds the main divisions of the terrain of prayer. The most fundamental is that between the paved roads of vocal prayer and the cross-country walks of mental prayer. Our journey is concerned only with mental prayer.

The rudimentary form of mental prayer is meditation. It occupies the first leg of the journey of mental prayer. It is followed by contemplation, which is composed of stages that occupy the remainder of the journey. A clear understanding of the difference between meditation and contemplation is the minimal equipment required for our imaginative journey through developing prayer.

Meditation is the form of prayer in which the predominant activity is discursive reasoning. Like a cow nourishing itself on that frail substance, grass, and going all day from one place to another to find more, the meditator is constantly going from one idea to another. Discursive reasoning is the process of examining ideas, and making deductions and connections and conclusions and assessments. Meditation leads to a unified vision of life, and felt values that move to personal commitment and action.

Contemplation is the form of mental prayer in which the predominant activity is an understanding gaze. The meditator is searching but the contemplator is finding. Like a roaring bulldozer, the meditator is forever rooting out another headful of ideas. Like all people who have found their treasure, the contemplator is gazing at some deep truth, or holding to some vision with love.

Contemplation is a mental process in which the mind is both in action and at rest. It is in action in knowing, but at rest in that it is not seeking in order to know, because it has already found. Contemplation is, therefore, not mental inactivity but mental superactivity. The contemplator leaps by an intuitional bound of the intellect to a prolonged possession of spiritual realities which meditation ploddingly struggles to reach and never really does.

Since contemplation is intuitional, and since the word *intuition* is a weasel word, I define it. Intuition is "the direct and immediate apprehension by a knowing subject of itself, of its conscious states, of other minds, of an external world, of universals, of values or of rational truths."[1] Intuition is to the mind what seeing is to the eye. A good example of intuition is the spontaneous grasp of the principle of contradiction: *a thing cannot be and not be under the same aspect at the same time.* Intuition is therefore not a mere thinking about non-material realities, but in some sense an experiencing of them.

The highest form of contemplation, which is mystical contemplation, helps to bring out its nature. In mystical prayer, there is experienced "a tranquil abiding in the presence of God"[2]; there may be the experience of "God uniting Himself directly to us."[3]

A concrete example of the difference between meditation and contemplation can be provided by imagining a walk through an art gallery. You stroll quietly through the display rooms, gazing meditatively on each of the paintings as you pass. You enter another chamber, and are immediately overwhelmed by one luminescent masterpiece. Your companion prods you, and only then do you realize that for an indeterminate amount of time, you had been lost in the one painting, and had not so much as been aware of the many others displayed in the room. You had been contemplating, but with the aid of the senses. Now substitute ideas and spiritual realities for the painting in the art gallery, and we have meditation and contemplation as they occur in prayer.

There is, of course, a problem of overlap. Every good prayer contains some contemplation, because every prayer has moments when we stop at least briefly to enjoy what we have found. The stages of prayer are named, however, not from a trace of an activity, but from a predominance of it. Meditators spends most of their time searching by thinking, though hopefully some part of their prayer each day is the joy of finding truth and faith and hope and love and the Beloved. But contemplators bypass all the preliminary work. They have done the necessary spadework in the past history of their life of prayer. The searching powers of reason are being given a well-earned rest. Reason has gradually come to understand the implications of the Christian revelation, and been converted bit by bit to accepting it fully and to esteeming it beyond all else; now it is content to let the contemplative power of the mind reach out to all that it has discovered, and even go beyond it to gaze on mysterious realities which reason had attained to by faith but could not climb to by thinking.

What should emerge from these reflections on the divisions of mental prayer is the basic characteristic of the change in prayer as one progresses. Prayer development is the movement toward the quiet of a superior inner activity.

It is a development away from primary involvement with the truths of God to communion with the God of truth. It is, therefore, a shift away from the visible spectrum of normal human perceptions to the ultra-violet of faith activity. Prayer is a work of two, and progress in prayer is an ongoing development of personalization that ultimately terminates in total union with God, whom the person of prayer addresses.

Ready for the Journey

Now that we know what to look for, we are ready to make our pilgrimage through developing prayer. Here now are the travelers whom we plan to accompany. They are being whisked out of their bustling metropolis by car. They catch hardly a glimpse of the smaller structures, but here a towering skyscraper looms up, and there workmen swarm over a new construction site. Their gaze flies from one object to another, just as the mind leaps from thought to thought in vocal prayer.

Soon the car reaches the outskirts of the city. Now more restful sights meet the eye. There are lovely suburban homes on spacious lawns, and open stretches where unruly grass and wild flowers grow. It is a pleasure to let the eye rest on each scene for the short span the speeding car allots.

The passage from city to suburb represents the transition from vocal prayer to the first stage of mental prayer, *meditation*. Each attractive suburban home is a thought which meditators turn over in their minds before discarding it for the next.

Meditation is the foundation of all mental prayer, for it Christianizes the reasoning powers. I will omit a description of it here since almost anyone reading this account will have personal experience of meditation. The main point is that in the meditative stage of mental prayer, thoughts are many and feelings are sparse.

In a reflective atmosphere such as a well-run novitiate, meditation commonly begins to metamorphose into the next stage of prayer within months after the meditator has mastered the art. We can gain insight into the changes by returning to our terrestrial travelers.

The car has reached the open countryside now. Spacious farmlands abound. An apple orchard with bright red fruit attracts the gaze. Farther along, golden waves of wheat are driven by the wind. Beauty is everywhere and its extensive dimensions invite a more protracted and reflective gaze.

Our journeyers through prayer have reached the *prayer of affection*. What has happened is that the meditators' thoughts and reasonings have grown deep and powerful enough to sweep feelings into the same orbit. First there are affections of all kinds—sorrow, fear, hope. Then there is affectionateness, growing love. Now at last the life of the feelings and affections is being Christified, too. The meditator is now beginning to live and labor for Christ with a certain amount of passion. This stage of prayer, too, is likely to be quite familiar to the reader, so I will omit a development of its characteristics.

Our terrestrial travelers have sped into the countryside by now. The farmlands have yielded to immense forests. They find the view monotonous at first, but gradually become more perceptive. What looked always the same begins to yield up its captivating secret of constant change dappling its unchanging constancy.

The Prayer of Simplicity

What has happened is that the journey through developing prayer has carried us beyond the prayer of affection into the *prayer of simplicity.* The prayer of simplicity is a milestone in prayer and so we must give it our full attention. We will begin by looking at this prayer in the perspective of our journey so far. Perspective will reveal to us that this stage is a natural outgrowth of the preceding ones.

In meditation, the first stage of mental prayer, we were predominately searching, and the workhorse was our reasoning power. When our reason began to mine deeply enough, they struck the pay dirt of our affections. They began to uncover our hidden loves. Our reasoning powers began to get some rest, as our heart began to awaken. This was the prayer of affection. Our affections led us to gaze more at length at the truths we had come to understand. The understanding gaze was in reality the first stirrings of contemplative prayer. Reasoning was just beginning to give way to intuitional activity. In the prayer of affection, then, the activity was split about fifty-fifty between the reason and the affections, and the higher intellectual activity known as intuition was just beginning to bud.

Only now as we enter the prayer of simplicity do we realize that we had been acting somewhat like excited children, rushing from one strike to another, grasping a handful of gold here and another there, when we could have settled down anywhere. The drilling power of reason has opened such inexhaustible veins of truth and affection that the only sensible thing to do is to stay in one place and mine there indefinitely. The understanding gaze of the intellect supplants the pick and shovel of reason in providing the material that stirs the heart.

Our pilgrims may only now discover how close and personal their relationship with Jesus can be. Or they may for the first time really discover Mary, or come alive to the presence of Jesus in the Blessed Sacrament. Again like a friend of mine, they may discover how incredibly Jesus reveals himself in Saint John's account of the Last Supper. They may return there day after day for months. In general, a person in this stage discovers one rewarding prayer relationship, and remains in it indefinitely.

The prayer of simplicity is almost too simple to describe— or too profound. What persons who reach simplicity have really discovered is love. They have been touched by the Holy Spirit. Within prayer, they find rest. They simply love, or, in simple words, make love. In the prayer of affection they had learned to love, but in the prayer of simplicity they fall in love. For five or ten minutes at a time, and even much longer, one thought grips, one affection grows. "The Lord is my shepherd, I shall not want; he makes me lie down in green pastures. He leads me beside still waters; he restores my soul"(Ps. 23:1-2).

Affections continue to grow stronger and more enduring, and this quiet new strength permeates not only our prayer but our lives. We are more peaceful now, less inclined to flare up, less moody. In prayer we may discover something about Jesus that we did not know, and our joy lasts for twenty minutes or twenty days. We find a new confidence in God through the words of scripture. We frequently come upon a passage that moves us deeply. The affection may subside partially, but a residue may remain the rest of our lives. One novice tried by desolation found help for a whole year running in Paul's irrefragable logic: "He who has not spared even his own Son but has delivered him for us all, how can he fail to grant us also all things with Him?" (Rom. 8:32). One truth haunts us, one affection possesses us. Our prayer and our lives are becoming single-minded. "I found him whom my heart loves. I took hold of him and would not let him go" (Song of Songs, 3:4).

Our mind, will, and affections have really been caught up in the mystery of Jesus. Our minds are steadier because steady gazing on one truth is bringing such great rewards.

The restless searching to and fro is over for now. The intellect is at long last finding what the heart really wants, and even the senses are at times flooded with joy in response to these interior experiences. The person who reaches the prayer of simplicity has finally reached the foothills of the mountain of contemplation.

In this stage the Gospels may take on a freshness and life we never dreamed they could have. Not only are they suffused with the glow of revelation, but God is addressing them to us personally. Many passages take on new meaning every time we read them, as though God were just writing them to cast light on the events of the day. And read the scriptures we ought, for now that meditative thinking has been squeezed out of our time of mental prayer, it normally takes place quite spontaneously while we read, and in spare moments during the day. "Where your treasure is, there is your heart also" (Matt. 6:21). If we do not nourish the prayer of simplicity by daily reading of the scriptures and other spiritual works, and by spiritual musings dispersed through the day, our prayer of simplicity may grow anemic and even die of starvation. This would drive us back along the way we have come, back to the hard work of grubbing in the fields of meditation (which are not half so attractive the second time round).

We grow and mature in many ways by the power of this prayer, which is to religion what a love affair is to life in the world. We could draw an analogy between life with God and falling in love in the natural world, and find a close parallel. Outside the formal hour of prayer, now, we long to return and be with Jesus. In a way, we are always with him. We do not always have the consolation of his presence, but yet we do everything rather conscious of God looking on. We are instantly aware of every selfish or sinful act by a kind of reflex examination of conscience, so that the appointed examen becomes simply a summary rather than a search, and we are able to spend much of the time allotted to it communing with Jesus. We are almost always searching for God in everything now by trying to please him in everything, and our thoughts are constantly turning to him. We are approaching the heartland of prayer.

Distractions

Distractions during this stage of prayer require our special attention. In some stages of prayer (even more advanced ones than this) distractions are frequently not blameworthy. In fact, some degree of distraction is inevitable: in the earlier stages, because the different powers of the soul are still unruly and unconverted to inner realities; and in later stages because some of the powers of the soul are left to themselves like orphan children while others are engaged with God. In the full-blown prayer of simplicity, however, the prayer is so engrossing and rewarding that distractions are a warning something is going wrong. We must look to the causes.

The causes of distraction (both those that are blameworthy and those that are not) do not change, no matter what our state of prayer. The first cause to suspect is a divided heart. A heart is divided by arranging our values according to wrong priorities, or by admitting into our lives conflicting values. In such a heart loves are not whole, and unwholesome love cannot survive. "No one can serve two masters"(Matt. 6:24).

What is most likely to cause a divided heart today? In answer, let me quote several lines from George Herbert's "Break of Day":

> Must business thee from hence remove?
> O, that's the worst disease of love.

> The poor, the foul, the false love can
> Admit, but not the busied man.

Must business thee from hence remove? Distractions "thee from hence remove." When distractions drag us away from a prayer of pure love like the prayer of simplicity, there is one thing to suspect: *ambition.* Ambitious persons (the "busied man") cannot love wholesomely because they are too in love with self and self-aggrandizement. Ambition is a shoal upon which prayer life—and even religious vocation—breaks to bits. The zeal, the industry, the overwork, and the professionalism to which religious are so often called today can subtly but readily degenerate into ambition. Activities that look virtuous, if they are eating away at our prayer, may only be the sickly signs of the success syndrome. The center of infection is *not* the determination to do what we prefer, but the determination to succeed in what we do. We begin well by accepting any assignment whatsoever. Once assigned, however, our will to success is stronger than our commitment to God's will and our fidelity to love. God can ask anything of us—except mediocrity or failure. We are determined to succeed in our projects even if the price is failure in life and love.

Fatigue is the second great enemy of prayer, and more so of advanced forms of prayer. On the surface, advanced forms appear effortless, and may even be experienced as effortless. Actually, however, this effortless activity involves an intense concentration of the intellect on a mental or spiritual reality. Like study, it cannot be done when one is exhausted, and if it is continued too long, it produces exhaustion, it "breaks heads." The famous mystical work, *The Cloud of Unknowing*, insists that advanced prayer requires restfulness, and counsels us to take good care of our health.

Other major causes of distraction are a failure to order our affairs properly outside of the time of prayer; a failure to live a life of recollection (for developing prayer *is* a state of greater and greater recollection); and a soul too small to measure up to the demands of love.

The Next Phase

We are on a journey, and the next phase is not far off now. The intensely attractive and rewarding prayer of simplicity may flourish at its peak for a year or more before the signs of decay set in, and the buds of an advanced form of prayer begin to swell. During that blessed interval, we may develop the same ardent relationship with Mary that we enjoy with Jesus, though the attendant division of our attentions will cause suffering. Then once again Jesus must become the center of our universe. Gradually, imperceptibly, the humanity of Jesus grows unobtrusive, perhaps by reason of merging with our own, and the rising star of his divinity claims our attention. Even if you watch a wheat stalk closely, you will not see it grow. No more do we observe this change, but the day comes when the One who permeates our whole prayer is true God of true God, the eternal Word. The human history of Jesus does not enter this world of the One who is ineffable, transcendent, divine and infinitely appealing—the source of all beauty and love and truth and goodness.

Soon after this the first of two difficulties may begin to appear. We start to lose taste for this beautiful prayer, vaguely aware that something is wrong. The second difficulty appears sporadically. We begin losing our power to pray the prayer of simplicity. We struggle to recover it, yet even when we succeed we are no longer satisfied. When we fail, we return to some former stage of prayer, but find the effort bitter and the results niggardly.

The danger is that these frustrations will lead us to give up, grow lax in prayer, and as the years pass, remember bitterly the progress we once made in the days when we could pray.

This plight underscores the need for a competent spiritual director, or at the very least a first-rate book on the stages of prayer like Dom Godefroid Belorgey's *The Practice of Mental Prayer* (The Newman Press, 1952).

We need knowledge of what is happening, to make the right response. To be specific, at this point we need to know the cause of the two difficulties, and the solutions to them.

The cause of the loss of taste for the beautiful prayer of simplicity need not be unfaithfulness of any kind. The loss can be a sign of progress. In the past, thoughts about God and attendant affections had been rewarding and Christifying. But as we approached God our prayer became less sensible, more spiritual. There were fewer ideas, fewer churnings of the mind. Not only can no idea contain God, but that earlier churning of the mind was like the stirring of the water in a pool just when we were trying to see to the bottom, see God.

When you fall in love, you are not satisfied with thoughts or images of the person. You want *presence.* So it is with persons of prayer who have been sated with thoughts of God by meditation, and sated with affections relating to God by the prayer of simplicity. They begin to feel oppressed by thoughts of God, not because they do not want God, but because they do. To think *about* God is to turn from God. *Pardon me, God, while I think about You.* They do not want to think *about* God but to *think God.*

It is time to stop looking for God within our own minds, as though God were a creature who could be embodied in an image and a thought. It is time to go off into the desert of the infinite to find God's very Self, without any image and without any thought. There is impatience with the ersatz of images because there is a felt need to communicate, have communion, unite and love-know the Lord God. "Show me Your glory!" (Ex. 33:18).

The second difficulty, the loss of power to pray the prayer of simplicity, may simply be that we have lost heart for the prayer because in the end God is not to be found in it; it may be that the grace for the prayer is being withdrawn to compel us to go on; it may be that God's new activity in us is interfering with our own, which ought to subside now.

At the onset of these difficulties, we still want to pray —we long for the hour of prayer. In the prayer, however, we seem to want to do *nothing*. We have entered into the *prayer of faith*.

The Prayer of Faith

We can be greatly helped at this time if we come across the words of Jesus recorded for us by John: "Whoever loves me will keep my word, and My Father will love him, and we will come to him and make our dwelling with him" (Jn. 14:23). We memorize these words and daily begin our prayer with them. Begin it? The words may be our whole prayer. Not that we keep repeating them. Rather, they are the staff on which our faith leans as we sit there doing nothing, content to be with God who has promised to be with us. We are not even trying to form a thought of God, for that would distract us from God. Truly, it is the prayer of faith.

If it sounds difficult, it is probably because it is difficult, unless we have great faith. There is a certain peace in what we do, but we are frequently tempted to unrest. *I want to be with You, God. I am with You, God. Or am I? Am I really praying or just wasting my time? Should I not be doing something?* There is much evidence that at this point many turn back. They find it safer to go back down to the lowlands of "sensible" prayer and look at God from a distance. They may be abetted in their cowardice by a cowardly or ignorant spiritual director.

A dear friend of mine, who seems to have been in this prayer of faith for years, used to ask me periodically, "What do you think? Am I *praying*?" And we would talk about it.

What is the answer to this question? When is a person ready and able to pray the prayer of faith? Various authors answer the question in basically the same way. Let me refer to Dom Godefroid Belorgey, since it is his teaching which is my chief source for this essay. He writes that we are ready for this prayer if 1) we have come to the point where we find discursive prayer fruitless and distasteful, and 2) we desire that our prayer be a simple abiding with God.[4]

Given these two signs in fervent persons, spiritual directors should encourage them to experiment with the prayer of faith when they profess the desire for it. If it is clear that their prayer life has evolved through the stages of meditation, the prayer of affection, and the prayer of simplicity, the evidence of readiness for the prayer of faith is all the more solid.

The spiritual director will confirm the decision by two further signs: success in the prayer, and profitable results such as a growing desire for God and growing abandonment to God's will.[5] These signs cannot be easily measured from a point in time. One must accumulate evidence over a period of months. Even outside of prayer there will be a subsiding of the emotions and a decreasing sense of reward in the daily activities, yet one will perform them with growing fidelity. They are for the Lord.

The difficulty with these signs is that they are ambiguous. What *is* success in prayer where nothing *appears* to be happening? One day we are convinced of our success, and the next day not. Faith waxes and wanes with our biological cycles. For that reason Saint John of the Cross gives us much bolder advice:

> When the spiritual person cannot meditate, let him learn to be still in God, fixing his loving attention upon Him, in the calm of his understanding, although he may think himself to be doing nothing ... And if, as we have said, such a person has scruples that he is doing nothing, let him note that he is doing no small thing by pacifying the soul and bringing it into calm and peace, unaccompanied by any act or desire, for it is this that Our Lord asks of us, through David, saying: "Be still and see that I am God."[6]

Note that Saint John addresses this advice to the "spiritual person." This is both an encouragement and a caution. An encouragement, since it is a generalized requirement which many fulfill. A caution, since it is clear that an ungenerous, unmortified person is ridiculous to presume to make this prayer which invites God to enter into union—in this case, into union with one who has refused union of wills with God.

If the signs are verified, the pilgrim has reached the austere prayer of faith. It is time to pray without thoughts, contemplatively, as once we prayed without contemplation, meditatively. It is time to treat thoughts as distractions, even meditative thoughts, even scriptural thoughts. During prayer, now, we must *put out thoughts without thought*. The reason is simple. Thoughts about God are not God. Now thoughts about God only distract us from God. We must develop the disciplined art of putting out thoughts without thought during the time of mental prayer.

The fruit of this prayer is priceless. By supernatural faith, the person's intellect clings to the unseen God; by supernatural love, the person's will actually embraces

God. This possession of God cannot be seen, tasted, touched, heard or smelled. But by faith it is known, and it is treasured beyond any former possession of God in prayer. To know that I possess God, and to rest in the knowledge of that possession, is more than everything else.

Once I hovered between life and death in a hospital bed. Day after day my mother would come and sit beside me. We rarely spoke, I rarely opened my eyes. There was virtually no measurable communication. Yet those days were one of the most profound communions with her I have ever had. The prayer of faith is like that.

Acquired Contemplation

The prayer of faith is *acquired contemplation*. It is the phase of prayer in which the intuitional powers of the soul are active by the aid of ordinary grace. We "see" God is with us, but we "see" only by faith. In this life the will, by the aid of supernatural charity, can actually reach out and touch God by love. The intellect, however, can only "blindly see" by faith. That is what it does in the prayer of faith.

The prayer is called *acquired contemplation* because it can be acquired by fidelity to the ordinary graces given the baptized. Without special graces, it is the highest pinnacle of prayer attainable. We have reached the end of the journey of ordinary prayer. To reach this Himalayan peak is all that human beings can do at their best. Further advance in prayer does not come about by pilgrims going higher, but by God coming lower. Across an unbridgeable gulf, not of space but of being, lies mystical prayer. "Be, my Beloved, like a gazelle, a young stag, on the mountains of the covenant" (Song of Sol., 3:17). Unless the divine lover leaps the abyss, it is only by faith that the intellect can know it already possesses what it longs for.

To reach this height of prayer, we have had to leave the lowland faculties of imagination and reason lying dormant below us. Without the wings of faith, even intuition, the loftiest act of the intellect, cannot rise to this plateau of being whereon God resides.

Without a readiness to die a kind of spiritual death, we will not perdure in the prayer of faith. Its preternatural dormancy is a crucifixion of the powers of the soul, which find their pleasure in activity. This prayer slowly and effectively purifies our sense faculties. It does in a slow, less violent way what the first dark night accomplishes in a mystical way. The first dark night, or dark night of the senses, purifies the senses and makes them marvelously submissive to a person's spirit, just as the second dark night makes the person's spirit marvelously submissive to God.

It is a disgrace to think of this prayer as a waste of time. It is time to stop thinking of mental prayer as primarily a time of meditation on divine truths, and to see it as a time of being with a divine person. It is time to stop thinking about time spent with a divine person as though it were time idly spent or selfishly spent. If even ordinary companionship develops and humanizes us, what development and superhumanization must germinate during the hours of this unique companionship? Contemplatives return *changed*, they return laden with the very gifts the world and the Church most need. The divine gift-giver would not think of letting them return empty-handed. It is not too much to say that they return *being* what the Church and world most need, *an opening through which God enters the world.* God does not enter the world through a vacuum, but through the being of one turned over completely to the Trinity.

Accompanying Troubles

We need further norms to guide us along this leg of the journey of prayer. Not only is the prayer of faith difficult to describe, but the troubles which attend it are difficult to catalog. To begin with, the prayer itself is a prayer of habitual dryness. If we return to our analogy, the terrestrial travelers, we discover a dramatic change. They are now passing through an interminable desert, burning and barren and motionless, save for the mirages playing on the super-heated sands. No relief is in sight anywhere. Dare they go on? Can they endure until the desert is crossed? And when will that be? The maps are not to scale, and no one knows. In the journey of prayer, it may be months, years, a lifetime.

Yet even here, the journeyers become acclimated. The breathless grandeur of the place slowly breaks in on them, so that they begin to say there is even something about it that they like. They would not have wanted to miss any of it. They even begin to feel at home!

One of the great difficulties in this stage is that it is plagued by states of *pseudo-prayer* which ape it. Yet, since the prayer of faith is true contemplation, there is a difference between *it* and the states aping it, however difficult it is to discern and describe the difference. Belorgey catalogs the difference with tremendously helpful precision through the use and description of his terms *obscurity* and *vagueness.*[7]

Obscurity is the prayer of faith in its dry purity. In the state of obscurity contemplatives experience nothing as long as they "do nothing" in the sense of not bringing any conscious thought or image before their minds. They are resting in God's presence *in faith*. Should they deliberately entertain a distraction, or take up a thought or a spiritual book, they feel a loss of peace. They may even feel a sense of guilt and betrayal. They are like an iron filing being pulled back to the divine magnet, and are resisting. Only let them go back where they belong, and they will feel nothing, and perhaps soon be tempted once again to stop "wasting time." Once again the rebuff will occur, and they will return willingly enough. The problem need not be unwillingness but only uncertainty resulting from weak faith or lack of knowledge concerning this stage of prayer.

It should be clear that in this condition of obscurity within the stage of the prayer of faith, contemplators should bravely screw up their courage and adhere to God by faith, doggedly persisting when hit by the shrapnel of distractions and discouragement. Substitute forms of prayer will be unsuccessful as well as distasteful or even repugnant. The only true course is to continue to return to God's obscure but tremendous presence.

Vagueness is another matter. It is a falling out of the prayer of faith. Victims of vagueness once prayed the prayer of faith and experienced the obscurity described above. Now, in time of prayer, they find themselves adrift, wandering anywhere at all, discovering no trace of God, and not feeling any reproach or any recall. They feel profane, lost and abandoned. They do not want to take up the practices of the past, but can find no future into which to advance. When they stubbornly try to rest in the faith that God is present, they drift into dangerous reveries as undisciplined as dreams. Even outside the time of prayer such reverie may assail them.

It should be clear that vagueness is an entirely different matter than obscurity. In vagueness we have lost the trail. Whether by fault or fatigue (always to be suspected), or by reason of loss of recollection as a result of the demands of life, we have fallen out of our purified state of faith-contemplation. We are athletes who have been struck down by sickness. We must once again go into training. We must return to one of our former states of prayer temporarily. Which state will succeed, we must learn by trial and error. We may have to resort to meditative reading as Saint Teresa of Avila had to do for so many years. It is a bitter regression, but pride will get us nowhere.

It is appropriate to point out here how we must consult the history of prayer to thread our own way through developing prayer. It is the part of pride not to consult the history of the saints. A book like Belorgey's, or Poulain's *The Graces of Interior Prayer* (B. Herder Co, 1911), represents a distillation of the revelation to the saints of prayer over the course of history. Such books also represent the experience of many other holy people, catalogued by their spiritual directors, and illumined by theological analysis. We need to resort to the collective experience of saints and theologians to make the most of the graces we receive and of our own effort.

Use of other forms of prayer may soon repel the vagueness and launch the contemplator once again into obscurity. It may be less work and more sleep that will do the trick. It may take a drive against habits of laxity, tepidity and soft living that have reasserted themselves now that the consolations of the prayer of simplicity are gone. We have to find out what will work and put it to work, perhaps again and again.

We can summarize in a few words the conduct appropriate to the prayer of faith: in obscurity, persist. In vagueness, resort to some other form of prayer, revitalize our fidelity and relieve any fatigue or poor health that may weigh the spirit down. Soon, prayer of faith should be possible again.

The Prayer of Quiet

Desert travel has parched and dulled our terrestrial travelers. It seems nothing can get worse. A little farther on the desert road begins a steep ascent and their car overheats. How much farther can they go? They top a sandy ridge—and a new world lies beneath! Rolling hills, scented and green, a lush valley cooly shaded, and the gently rolling waves of a vast inland sea. The desert is all behind them now.

Is there an analogous reprieve for parched contemplators buffeted between obscurity and vagueness? Happily, there can be.

One day they are sterilely ploughing through the cloud of obscurity, with nothing different than it has been for months and years. Or perhaps they are not even engaged in formal prayer. They are about their ordinary affairs. *Then God is there!* They have no proof, but it does not even occur to them to doubt. It is God. God was not expected, God could not be brought, but God has come. This visitation is the prayer of quiet. It is an interior experience of God, not as a vision, but as a felt presence.

Because this initial experience of the prayer of quiet does not well illustrate the reason for its name, another (usually more advanced) experience of the prayer of quiet will be added here. One makes a last visit to the Blessed Sacrament for the day, returns to one's room, and reaches for the light switch to retire. In the darkness, a quiet descends on oneself and everything present, and the dark is a part of the quiet, and light would be noise. The quiet permeates body and soul through and through. Senses, desires, spirit have never been quiet like this. Surprise! This Quiet is not a lack but a presence. *This quiet is someone. "It is the Lord!"* (Jn. 21:8). The divine Friend had decided to pay another visit, unannounced. Instinctively, the pilgrim says nothing, becomes part of the quiet, dwells in silent communion with the divine Guest, as one who has unknowingly been in training for this silent role. When sleep comes, the quiet is still there. An awakening in the night finds the soul attended still. In the morning, the quiet is gone, and the vagueness has returned. This visitation is simply a more pronounced experience of the prayer of quiet.

We have reached the next leg on the journey. It is true mystical prayer. This can be seen simply by consulting the definition of Poulain, who defines the mystical as "those supernatural acts or states which our own industry is powerless to produce, even in a low degree, even momentarily."[8]

Like all forms of *mystical* contemplation, this contemplation is *passive*, because it is an experience which the subject cannot originate or terminate. It begins when God comes, and ends when God leaves. God comes and goes, not by changing position, but by changing relationship with us through a momentary interior grace. Still, there is no other word for it than *visit.* Like any other friend, only more sovereignly, God comes and goes at the divine good pleasure.

One act does not make a state. Persons who receive such a visit may remain in the prayer of faith indefinitely. Still, they will never be the same again. They have been in the presence of the Beloved. Fidelity to the memory of God's visitation will be strength for the journey through darkness until God comes again.

This experience of God is no bolt of lightning or searing vision. Yet it changes everything. Outside of prayer, the contemplator cannot find the world. It has turned to dust and ashes. What is it compared to God? Inside of prayer, God cannot be found.

The prayer of faith may continue for years, marked by an occasional visitation of God in the prayer of quiet. For some, however, the transition into the state of quiet may proceed more quickly and permanently. Contemplators who advance into the fullness of the prayer of quiet will frequently or even habitually experience God. In the prayer of faith they had the certitude of faith that God was present, but in the prayer of quiet they have the *feeling* of God's presence. The Presence impresses itself on them. They can no more cause or remove that Presence than the ear can hear or not hear at will. It is, however, often a much more subtle presence than the one above described at the onset of this prayer, and easily yields to distractions. In this stage prayer consists in giving one's attention to God in non-verbal communication.

There are stages beyond the prayer of quiet, though few seem to reach them. In the prayer of quiet, God unites himself with the power of the will (the power to love). The next stage is that of *full union*. In full union, the intellect, too, is taken up into the embrace. Even the senses are partially absorbed in the union, so that a person praying in this state can be oblivious to the passage of time.

The stage beyond full union is called *ecstatic union*. Now the person is so lost in God that virtually all contact with the outer world is suspended during prayer. God must terminate the prayer because the contemplator is a captive of his presence.

If the final stage is to be reached, the second dark night descends on the soul to detach it from all remaining things and teach it absolute submission to God. When the purgation has prepared it, it advances to the final stage of the journey, the *spiritual marriage*. "By a clear and distinct view, the soul now sees how it is indissolubly wedded and united to God."[9]

Let love impel one to make this long, vast, and arduous journey to God, and little by little one will enter into union with the Lord. There will be difficulties, but I cite Belorgey's universal remedy: "No matter what our state, then, if we have lost God, let us pray. For in this we shall find him again!"[10]

This highly imperfect and inaccurate road map of the journey of prayer cannot be considered adequate for the traveler, but it can do one thing. It can assure us from the experience of the many on whom it draws that the Son of God was serious when he said: "Look, I am standing at the door, knocking. If one of you hears me calling and opens the door, I will come in to share his meal, side by side with him" (Rev. 3:20).

Notes

[1]Dagobert D. Runes, *Dictionary of Philosophy* (Totowa, N.J., Littlefield, Adams & Co., 1967), article "Intuition."

[2]Karl Rahner and Herbert Vorgrimler, *Theological Dictionary* (New York, N.Y., Herder and Herder, 1965), article "Contemplation."

[3]Louis Bouyer, *Dictionary of Theology* (Desclee & Co., 1965), article "Mysticism."

[4]Dom Godefroid Belorgey, O.C.S.O., *The Practice of Mental Prayer* (Westminster, Md., Newman Press, 1952), p. 57.

[5]Belorgey, p. 57-8.

[6]*The Works of Saint John of the Cross* (Westminster, Md., Newman Press, 1945), trans., E. Allison Peers, p. 129.

[7]Belorgey, p. 70.

[8]R. P. Poulain, S.J., *The Graces of Interior Prayer* (St. Louis, Mo., B. Herder Co., 1911), p. 1.

[9]Belorgey, p. 162-3.

[10]Belorgey, p. 138.

Chapter Two

Prayer and Personality Development

Herbert F. Smith, S.J.
V. Michael Vaccaro, M.D.

"A Pilgrimage Through Prayer" presents a bird's-eye view of the most traveled thoroughfare through developing prayer as vouched for by Saints of prayer who have made the journey. Here, we will look at the same stages of ascending prayer, to observe the signs and causes of personality growth at each level.

Is there a causal connection between growth in mental prayer and personality development? Some consider the question a prostitution of prayer. But we should learn all we can about prayer and personality. If prayer develops personality, we need the knowledge to respond to those who attack prayer as a regressive infantilizing of personality. More important, if personality is that unique selfness out of which each of us gives an individual response to God, a failure to grow is a failure to become capable of the response God desires. If each stage of prayer develops qualities which dispose us for the next stage, it is worth knowing what those qualities should be, to facilitate their cultivation and to cooperate better in the ascent of prayer.

What is personality? In the most popular sense, personality is "a distinction or excellence of personal or social traits." More profoundly, it is "the quality or state of being a person," and "the complex of characteristics that distinguishes an individual," especially "the totality of an individual's behavioral and emotional characteristics."[1]

More profoundly still, and more to our purpose, "In an ethical sense, personality may be said to be present when a human being's free decision really and unflinchingly accepts the fact that he is a person: accepts the dialogical character of life ordered to mystery, accepts freedom, duty, responsibility, unrepressed sinfulness, his neighbor's ineffable individuality, pain, and death. Complete personality is rooted in the genius of the heart, not the intellect."[2] If, then, personality is most fundamentally the quality of being a person, it is "to possess oneself as a subject in conscious, free relation to reality as a whole and its infinite ground and source, God."[3]

In defining personality, we should also call to mind the empirical elements which participate in personality formation: genetic, familial, religious, cultural, social, political. This recall acknowledges that, while human personality is essentially rational and free, it emerges out of human experience. One's experience may limit, and indeed impede, the development of personality, maturity, or free expression. On the other hand, it is precisely in the struggle to overcome such natural impediments that the individual personality may develop further and, in the process, lean on and enhance the growth of prayer life.

What is the relationship between personality and character? Character is the complex of intellectual, affective, behavioral and ethical traits marking and individualizing a person. It manifests the essence of personality. So, in tracing prayer's influence on the development of personality, we will be tracing its influence on the development of character as well.

Psychological Developments Antecedent to Prayer

The formation of personality and character traits that antedate the beginnings of prayer life both contribute to and impede prayer's influence on personality. So, to set the stage for our study of prayer and personality development, we need to consider those antecedents.

Every child is born with positive and negative qualities predisposing it to its own unique way of behaving. These qualities begin to shape personality long before reason matures to the point where the child becomes a free human agent of its own development. In these early years, parents and other mentors act as surrogates for children's undeveloped reason. Development at this stage will be good and rational only to the extent that the guidance provided is wholesome. In real life, surrogates deform as well as form children.

Impulses produced by early personality formation include some which originate in the unconscious and are generally inaccessible to our understanding or even our consciousness. We act them out without really adverting to the fact, and we tend to carry them with us through life. As we pray and meditate, we may begin to realize how unfreely we are governed by certain of these impulses—though people close to us may long since have realized this. We smooth off the rough edges of the conduct the less desirable of these impulses produce, such as irascibility or neurotic oversensitivity but, generally, we do not come to an understanding of or control of their unconscious roots even in prayer. That is not necessarily a failure on our part, but may be a limitation of nature or grace.

As far as we can trace it, personality growth through prayer proceeds by the use of intelligence and free will, and their influence upon our affectivity. The influence of grace is generally hidden within the operation of these two spiritual faculties.

A basic hypothesis of depth psychology maintains that all psychic activity—and therefore prayer life—is qualified by early experiences. For example, impaired or distorted primitive development of conscience (i.e., superego development) will inevitably produce an immature conscience with myriad forms of moral dysfunction.

Oral, anal, phallic, and genital stages of personality growth can influence our conduct for life, and thus our prayer. The mental prayer we will be discussing develops after personality has sunk its roots. It will, therefore, be helpful to review the phases of childhood growth, and to note examples of the neurotic disorders which can spring from unhealthy childhood experiences. In the oral phase of infancy (the first year and a half), desires and gratifications are primarily oral. Deprived of the normal healthy experiences of the oral phase, a child will be impeded in its progress to the next phase. This can mark the child's later character with the neurotic qualities of the *hysteric:* flightiness, instability, nervousness, apprehensiveness, and sexual immaturity.

In the anal phase (from a year and a half to three years), the most important gratifications are anal. Too early or severe toilet training, followed by consequent repressions and character regressions, can lead to the *compulsive:* inhibited, overly self-controlled, and depressive.

In the phallic phase (beginning about the third year), children are fascinated by their genitals. Further healthy development leads to the genital stage, the stage of puberty, in which normal adult sexual organization, attitudes and interests blossom. Unhealthy experiences preventing transition from the phallic phase can result in the *phallic-narcissistic:* buoyantly—even arrogantly—self-confident, vigorous, athletic, and freighted with tendencies to homosexuality.[4]

Even a lay person's knowledge of such psychological analysis of personality problems can provide a glimmer of understanding in difficult cases. Without diagnosing specifics, spiritual guides can begin to understand why they fail in correcting certain evident faults in themselves and others, and why growth in certain directions seems blocked. Such failings may be due not to a lack of effort or good will, but to unconscious impulses; at times such failings are not even perceived. Having faced up to the role of unconscious impulses, spiritual guides adjust to character limitations in themselves and others. They begin to see how psychological literature may enrich self-understanding, spiritual direction, and formation. Where disturbances in their charges are severe, they will be alert to possible need for psychological counseling.

The lesson? As we trace the many ways in which mental prayer forwards personality development, *we will not expect it to undo the personality malformations which a person brings with him to prayer.* Handicapped persons might submit to athletic training, and such training might enable them to do much they could not otherwise accomplish, but in most cases it will not cure handicaps. Similarly, ordinary graces of the spiritual life may not work miracles, but they may help us surmount all psychic disabilities. This chapter will simply report what God normally does through prayer, not what he may choose to do in unique instances.

A notable caution! Contemporary psychology is, as said above, an important source of knowledge about character development. But in psychological literature, sublimation—a key factor in character development—is defined in accord with the psychological determinism of Freud: "an unconscious process whereby the libido, or sex instinct, is directed or transformed into a more acceptable form of outlet."[5] Wilhelm Reich, for instance, views character development as a *deleterious* process: He envisions character development as a rigid set of alterations which the ego mounts to repress wholesome actions that would lead to rejection by society or even by the socially-trained self. Sublimation, in this view, is really a degrading of pure psycho-sexual energies into inferior outlets. Reductively, Reich holds that the truly admirable person would be the characterless person, but the taboos of society prevent any such person from arising.[6] Unfortunately, this pernicious concept of sublimation prevails in depth psychology.

Depth psychology deals exclusively with psychic determinism, which is an unconscious process. It treats of human beings as animals, not as rational animals. It never comes to grips with the true nature of human beings.

The Christian tradition—and that of most if not all peoples—insists on giving primacy to the conscious, rational, and spiritual ego-determinants of character formation, growth and development. These are the mental powers which come to grips with the fundamental realities of objective good and evil, and provide the capability of discerning and freely choosing between them. Of course, these powers are often in conflict with the forces of the unconscious processes, and with the impulses that originate from original sin and all sin in the world, so that discernment and choice can be difficult.

In Christian asceticism, consciously-chosen sublimation is the free re-direction of lower impulses from commonplace satisfactions to the attainment of objectively higher values of unity, truth, goodness, beauty and charity and, ultimately, to the attainment of God and his promise of eternal life.

This fully human concept of sublimation will underlie our assessment of personality development, which derives so much from the use of the powers of intelligence and free will. The child must await the development of these powers to begin the process of appreciating transcendental values, and of judging between objective good and evil.

If the child's personality development continues without crippling trauma or dysfunction, the emergence of the capacity to reason will help the child respond to guidance in overcoming more base proclivities, and develop consistency in right actions until good habits are formed. Good habits in turn train and habituate the lower faculties of the psyche to conform to the movements of the higher faculties. At this point, sublimated activity, begun as hardship, can become pleasurable. (Pleasure, according to Aristotle, is the accompaniment of a perfect act.)

From a traditional vantage point, sound character is a largely-freely-chosen-and-developed habitually active synthesis of rational convictions, beliefs, values, affects, virtues and social attributes by which a person perceives, judges, and acts to attain worthwhile goals realistically chosen. In psychological terms, we develop sound character by ego-directed (that is, consciously directed) personality development.

Remnants of personality malformations remain in the unconscious, but sound character development will attenuate their effects, and sound character is what many of us hope to achieve.

Now to the role mental prayer may play in development of this desired personality

Growth of Personality in the Stage of Meditation

If we may allegorize in a fashion lent color by the writings of St. Teresa of Avila, to take up mental prayer is to enter a new world peopled by a tribe with its own unique evolutionary laws. Evolution, in this tribe, is a process which develops not over eons, but in each single lifetime. Here, not the phylum but the individual evolves into higher life forms, as is the case with caterpillars. They have long fascinated Christian believers because they metamorphose into sleeping chrysalises, and then into soaring butterflies, as we hope to pass through the sleep of death into the glory of the resurrection body.

Application of this concept of evolutionary development to prayer has a basis in the analogy of being: All things have some likeness to God their Creator, and therefore to one another. Use of analogy, carefully done, inspires insight. St. Teresa of Avila described the stages of prayer in terms of the rooms of a castle; here the description is in terms of the modern concept of evolution.

At birth, a tribal member is unable to pray. Prayer is learned with growth: first, vocal prayer, then mental prayer, of which meditation is the first stage. If we proceed in mystical evolution, we will soar up to higher and higher forms of prayer. The call to go on from stage to stage is deep and personal, and here a principle of the nature of growth in prayer begins to appear: The "call" is inner growth, and this growth is the call. Development in prayer and in personality are that closely intertwined. And in part, at least, personality development is a result of growth in prayer. To move on before being called is to climb out of the sea without lungs. Such a creature must get back into the sea fast or die of asphyxiation.

To present the growth of mental prayer under this allegorical form is to assert that there is an intrinsic relationship between personal growth and progress in mental prayer. By a spiritual instinct, the person of prayer moves on when growth bestows the competence for, and the attraction to, the more advanced spiritual activities.

We join our pilgrim as he passes from vocal prayer into the first stage of mental prayer, which is meditation. Meditation is mental prayer in which the predominant activity is discursive reasoning. It is a process of examining scripture and doctrine, of making connections and conclusions, inferences and assessments. In a way, it is a homely form of theologizing, mixed with outbursts of prayer.

Meditation is a personalized form of thinking and learning. For some persons at least, it is the first concentrated, perduring and habit-forming experience in thinking and, therefore, it is growth. Classroom learning tends to pass quickly into the memory as into a storeroom, so that the student learns the facts, but may not learn to think; meditative learning tends to steep in the mind and germinate in the will, and become part of the personal dynamic.

Christian meditation personalizes thinking in other ways. It concentrates on truths of utmost personal importance: on one's own nature and ultimate meaning as known by reason and revelation; on the mysteries of God and creation and the call to be companion and disciple of Christ in the work of the kingdom of the Father.

Dormant psychic energies are awakened. The vision of cosmic purpose acts like sunlight and rainfall on the seeds of one's gifts and talents, and they bear fruit. One discovers with interior clarity "the vocation of applying to the building up of the Church and to its continuing sanctification all the powers which (one) has received from the goodness of the Creator and from the grace of the Redeemer."[7]

This is nothing less than the awakening, or at least a more electrifying awakening, of personal significance. We thrill to the discovery of our meaning and potential. Our will power, gaining strength in meditative deliberation, pursues the discovered purpose.

A two-fold development of personality is in progress. The first is authentic growth in the use of reason and will which all persons share; the second is growth in personal uniqueness which comes from responding, out of one's own unrepeatable constellation of gifts and experiences, to one's personal call. The seal of solidity is stamped on this growth by the knowledge of self and the world which develops in sound mental prayer.

But progress is not made without struggle. Real obstacles to growth and service, which become so evident in meditation, tend to sap our courage to go on. Meditation on personal and cosmic sin can loose demons of alarm and depression with which we must deal. This is fundamentally healthy. Progress into reality is good, though initially it can be daunting.

In this conflict, the brave dig deep foundations in the soil of reality. Jung writes that it seems to be a sin in nature to hide insufficiency.[8] Sin and insufficiency are part of our makeup, and for health's sake must be raised to consciousness. Karen Horney finds the root of neurosis in an unconscious refusal to see this personal duality of health and sickness, ability and limitation, goodness and evil. Repressing awareness of the dark side, exaggerating the light side, and conceiving an Ideal Self which neither is nor can be—this is the neurotic pattern. A neurotic is unconscious of his or her Actual Self with its real strengths and weakness and bonds of neuroticism. Tragically, neurotics waste prodigious energies supporting the illusionary Ideal Self, and repressing awareness of the Actual Self—reducing it to a hated "omnipresent stranger" hovering on the horizon of consciousness and challenging all illusion. Trampled on and unacknowledged by these two antagonists is the Real Self, "the 'original' force toward individual growth and fulfillment," the Self which becomes manifest and vital when we are free of the shackles of neuroticism.[9]

When defenses break down, the neurotic person goes from seeing an Ideal Self to seeing a hopelessly depraved self: "I'm no good, never was, and never will be." (One psychiatrist maintains he never had a patient who did not have a rotten self-image.)

Both the delusion of the Ideal Self and of the Hopelessly Corrupt Self are corruptions of Christian teaching. Scripture stresses relentlessly both our failings and our strengths. Man is an obstinate sinner, yet "You have made him little less than godlike" (Ps. 8:6).

The neurotic pattern, common as the cold, warns us of the need for unyielding honesty and realism in mental prayer. To grow, we dig out rather than cover over our weaknesses, sins and sinfulness; with equal objectivity we uncover our strengths and gifts and graces.

Failure to face our weaknesses, limitations, and sinfulness warps our faith-call to holiness and loving service into a deluded vision of an Idealized Self, and our energies into neurotic efforts to cling to this vision. Alternately, when the vision is routed by reality, we are inclined to see nothing *but* our negative side, and resign ourselves to helplessness and hopelessness. In both cases we neglect the call to develop the Real Self and our real grace-call.

St. Paul shuns these traps: "I do not think of myself as having reached the finish line. I give no thought to what lies behind, but push on to what is ahead" (Phil. 3:13).

Prayer helps us to grow, but even by our best efforts to cooperate with God's grace we do not fully escape neuroticism. What we can do, with the aid of ego-directed action and grace, is come to the point where the positive and constructive elements of our personality are dominant over our neurotic elements (Any further dealing with neurotic traits may require psychotherapy.) Carried to excess, the kind of reflection we are making here leads to too much navel-gazing in meditation. It is common, it is harmful, and the answers don't lie in our navels. Only the companionship of Christ provides solutions; the Gospels are the best source of meditation. And even there, the wise pilgrim of prayer concentrates on Christ. "I am the way."

Meditation is a land of fireflies. Flashes of light delight the intellect and momentarily warm the heart. And so we grow. For thinking leads to judging truths, and judging to assessing values, and discovery of values to esteeming, feeling and loving them, and committing our lives to them—or rather, to Christ who teaches them.

Months and years of using the pick and shovel of meditation form habits of reason and insight, deepen faith and develop intellect. Attention no longer flits restlessly; it gazes reflectively. This contemplative gaze stirs hearts deeply because it sees deeply. The firefly flashes are turning to camp fires at which we pause to gather warmth before moving on to further thoughts. Notice, here, then the first stirrings of contemplative prayer.

Personality Development in the Prayer of Affection

Now we return to our image of mental prayer as a mythical land where an evolutionary process transpires in each member of the tribe. Our tribal member has spent the required time in the stage of meditation. Rational powers have grown and been Christianized. A subtle call signals that it is time to join the tribal members who have gone on to a higher stage, where the affective life burgeons. This stage is known as the prayer of affection. The pick and shovel of meditation, which used to uncover thoughts that satisfied primarily the mind, have dug down to a second level, into a layer of treasures that stir the affections. Reason, appreciator of the truth of things, is finding companionship of the heart, responder to the goodness of things seen by the mind. The thoughts now unearthed light up fires of affection across the landscape.

Emotional satisfaction, formerly produced mainly by sense experience, now commonly originates from judgments of reason. The spiritual powers of the soul are advancing the integration and harmony of the intra-psychic faculties.

Religious truth is putting on the passions of the heart. Before, the pushcart of the will had to translate faith into action; now it finds help in the draft animals of the emotions. Drawn by these powerful creatures, the pilgrim moves more swiftly into both praying and living the faith.

Mental health flourishes, for repressed and conflicted emotions, which are the roots of many health problems, are finding expression and even resolution. Daily life acquires new tone. Tenderness and sweetness flow into more gracious living. Joys and sorrows and other passions and affections bloom with greater spontaneity and psychological freedom.

All, however, is not idyllic. Growth has its problems. Something of a Pandora's box has been opened. Emotional liberation opens the gates on both the good and bad moods and emotions, and they go on holiday together— and not all holidays are good holidays. Passionate arguments, outbursts, whole troops of feelings can emerge. Fuller control of this richness lies in the future. Let us realize that if and when we gain sufficient dominance over these neurotic energies, we can not only restrain them but even direct them into useful channels. All our energies can be enlisted in the service of growth.

A pilgrim's budding contemplative mood often cloaks thought and insight in affections and moods that reward prayer's effort. The engendered warmth and tenderness, joy and gentle sorrow invite rest from work, to take spiritual nourishment from what has been found.

The affective life is maturing and Christifying. The Scriptures, which may have been dull, provide passages which glow and sing. Those whose affective lives were repressed or under-developed find an awakening; those who came with rich affective lives find them growing less shallow and excitable and sense-bound; they find them taking root in substances of greatness.

Imaginative contemplation is important in this stage because the imagination has great power to feed the prayer of affection, and it should be integrated into the growth process. Imaginative contemplation is prayer in which we replay events of the life of Jesus with the power of the imagination. For instance, it consists "in seeing in imagination the way from Nazareth to Bethlehem" which Joseph and Mary traveled. It concentrates on "seeing the persons, namely, our Lady, St. Joseph, the maid, and the Child Jesus after His birth." It goes yet further: "I will make myself a poor unworthy little slave, and as though present, look upon them and contemplate them, and serve their needs."[10] Notice how far St. Ignatius goes. He wants us to go back two thousand years, to be there, to play a part in the event. What is the value of imaginatively reconstructing the events of Salvation History? It has many values. God has given us imagination to escape the present and range through time, reconstructing what has been, and foreseeing what may be. Einstein praised imagination as more important than information. It sees possibilities and solves problems. It is often employed to sin; it can be employed to pray and to find and do God's will.

Some avoid imaginative contemplation, because their faculty of imagination is stunted. Perhaps all it needs is exercise, and they should try using it in prayer. Of course, there are people like St. Teresa of Avila, who wrote that her efforts to use her poor imagination brought her no help.

Some shun use of imagination because their reconstructions may be inaccurate. If Shakespeare were so faint hearted, we would not have *Romeo and Juliet,* and if St. Ignatius were so timid, his *Spiritual Exercises* would limp.

Prayer of affection develops and Christianizes the affective life and imagination. When they have reached some preordained degree of maturity, the native of the land of mental prayer senses the summons to pass on to the next stage of evolution.

Personality Development in the Prayer of Simplicity

Transition to the prayer of simplicity occurs, like the maturation process in general, gradually and non-dramatically. In the prayer of affection a multitude of affections may blossom one after the other in any hour of prayer, but now one deeply-rooted affection tends to rise and hold sway. If, in the last stage, natives of the land of prayer learned about love, in the prayer of simplicity they are becoming lovers. Promised is the development gained only by those who fall simply, selflessly, hopelessly in love. "I drew them with human cords, with bands of love (Hos. 11:4).

In prayer, the pilgrim dwells on one Gospel episode, is haunted by one truth, possessed by one affection. The relationship with the Lord is taking on the color of intimacy. With the disciples, the pilgrim participates in the Gospel events, hears the Lord's words, shares his values, feels the pulse of his life drawing closer.

Flurries of affection are yielding to moods of affectivity which hold sway consciously for days, and, more unobtrusively, in permanence. Affectivity can reach an ardor almost impossible to describe or exaggerate. The passive-receptive experience is felt in all its joy: Active now is the child's power to attract love, fused with an adult's gift of returning it in all its depths and consequences. Reflect here that, in general, development in prayer is movement from activity to passivity. That simply reflects the nature of contemplation (which is the restful gaze at truth or goodness or the beloved), and of love, which is a passion. We do not create it. It is an innermost welling up, the heart's response to the contemplated object.

Growth extends to all the reaches of the personality. The sensual part of the soul, tasting of the pleasures overflowing the intellect and the will in their contact with God, advances further into a life less dependent on the external senses. It is entering a deeper unity with the higher faculties.[11] The person is becoming more unified in himself, as he longs to become united with God.

The experience of love, like flooding light overpowering darkness, quells the cynicism about love so common in today's culture. Pilgrims discover a new freedom, the freedom for the unimpeded generosity of those who are loved. They have come to know the Truth—that is, the Beloved—and the Beloved has set them free.

The use of this freedom? "Sacrifice and sin offering you have not desired, but a body you have prepared for me" (Hebr. 10:5). They feel themselves wanted, called to incarnate Christ, as Christ incarnated God, and so to return in the Son to the Father by patterning their lives after the Son's. "As it is written of me in the book, I have come to do your will, O God" (Hebr. 10:7). At the root of this new vitality is a deeper knowledge of God gained from love. "*Amor est magis cognitivus quam cognitio* (We know better by love than by knowledge)," says St. Thomas Aquinas. This is illustrated by a theologian who can talk profoundly about God, yet experience no devotion and no conversion. But let that theologian, like St. Thomas, be given a touch of God and a sense of God's love, and he or she will experience a heart taking flame and a call to conversion. It is only the experience of love received and given that infuses an intimate knowledge of God. Human experience in and out of prayer confirms this mystery of the transforming power of love.

Out of this intimacy of love issues a growing sorrow for sin. Such growth is one of the surest signs of the authenticity of any grace. Sins of weakness, as infidelities to love, break the heart. "He went out and began to weep bitterly" (Mt. 26:75). Deliberate sin wrenches the whole personality.

We are treating of what, to the status-quo mind, sounds excessive, but Karl Stern says rightly:

> God loves man with the madness of love, and he tries man's love to the point of madness. It is the only way we can understand the story of a jealous, angry God of the Old Testament... It is a mad story, and those who get involved in it are affected by divine madness. 'God is a devouring fire.'[12]

Those who try to tame the human-divine relationship with logic and syllogism cannot well envision, much less enter, the prayer of simplicity.

The love bursting out in the prayer of simplicity develops another strength in pilgrims, the strength to respond heroically to their unique personalities and callings. Most people are too afraid of others to give that response. But love, like genius, resists the leveling process. Counter arguments and mores ("It isn't done") fall on deaf ears. The passionate lover follows the call of the beloved, and our pilgrim has become the passionate lover.

Personality Development in the Prayer of Faith

The siren song of the next stage of this spiritual evolution now begins. It rises like a gentle breeze that stirs the strings of a pilgrim's heart with new longing. It is the call to a new prayer, and to the development it requires. The pilgrim's inner powers have arrived at the foothills of a more rarified contemplation. What is happening is that the meditations, truths of faith and imaginative and affectivity experiences so rewarding up to this point, do not now suffice. Such activities will of course, continue throughout life, but at present they are being thrust out of the time of formal prayer. The intellect is no longer satisfied to gaze on ideas and concepts of God and of Jesus, because the gulf between the journeyer and the Lord is now felt as too vast to be bridged by these means. These thoughts and their accompanying sentiments feel as unwelcome and encumbering as a backpack on a runner.

An analogy: Imagine the Queen of Sheba hearing of King Solomon and eager to learn more. At length, she obtains a painting of him and it becomes a great favorite. The more she hears of him, the more his image fascinates her. Then a change sets in. The very sight of the painting creates a painful awareness of how little she knows about this wise and marvelous man. This will not do! She must meet him! She sets out on her journey to Jerusalem.

Pilgrims here are in a similar mental state. Everything that prayer offers is like Solomon's painting to the Queen of Sheba. It only stresses the gulf between them and their desire. They would trade it all for a sure and certain conviction that the Lord is present—even if they can't experience that presence. The prayer of simplicity has done all it can: It has inspired a longing for a higher reality—communion and union.

This sense of encumbrance and longing is the summons to the next stage of evolution, the prayer of faith. Of course, pilgrims don't recognize it as such. They are only aware that the prayer of simplicity, which was so lovely and wonderful, seems to lead to a dead-end. Driven by dissatisfaction, they seek something more in prayer, some other way. Grace and instinct help them, sooner or later, to discover scriptural passages which voice the call they feel:

"Be still and know that I am God" (Ps. 46:10). Be still! Desist! As the reasoning powers shift toward neutral in the prayer of simplicity, so the affections grow still in the prayer of faith.

This strange advance has light shed on it by those words of St. Thomas Aquinas, "The act of faith has as its term not faith statements but faith's goal, God" (*Actus fidei terminatur non in propositionem sed in rem.*) Anyone who makes an act of faith is, in that act, reaching out and attaining God the Almighty. Here we are in direct relationship to God, not by a statement, but by the touch of the intellect in the first moment of the act of faith. That touch is now craved by the will which, fired by love, wants to reach and embrace God.

In this life we cannot see God, but we can abide with him, and, when love is great enough, that is everything. "One who loves me will keep my word, and my Father will love him; we will come to him and make our home with him" (Jn. 14:23). In this stage, the desire to be with God which has always been there takes on a passion that can no longer be denied. It is this escalated intensity which has driven the pilgrim beyond the borders of the prayer of simplicity.

Prayer, at this time, takes the form of bolstering conviction of God's presence (with the help of such passages as Jn. 14:23) and resting in the Presence like a blind person sitting silently in a room with the beloved. Such prayer is austere and profound.

The nature of the personality growth promised by this stage both eludes the chronicler's pen and makes cruel demands on a spiritual wayfarer. One whose character stands up to the demands grows. Where character erodes under such duress, it falls back and suffers regression: It has met a call and a challenge to which it does not measure up.

What is required in this stage is an intellectual act which human powers cannot bring to its term. Even the most primitive act of faith cannot be made without the grace of God, for none can reach God in any way except by divine assistance. In minutes and hours and years of prayer, the pilgrim is called to act and persevere in action which is radically dependent on grace to reach its finality: Emmanuel, God with us. This is not a transient act of faith-assent, but prayer-periods of enduring intellectual gaze at the unseen Presence. It attains to God, but appreciation of this fact is another act of faith. Prayer has become a towering act of faith which leaves the intellect feeling wounded, inadequate, helpless.

What of personality growth in this austere prayer? The first element of growth is the advance to acquired contemplation (as distinct from passive contemplation which is produced only by mystical grace). The intellect is being honed to its finest natural achievement, in an act that has no rewarding spillover into the sensual faculties, as commonly takes place in the earlier stages, where the intellect delights in its insights, the imagination in its constructs, and the feelings through their participation in what has been thought and envisioned. That is why this prayer is called *arid*.

The second element of growth is the development of the will through its austere exercise in faith. The way had been prepared: love—which flowered in the prayer of simplicity—has produced new seeds of faith. What is faith but strength of mind, strength of will, strength of character, strength of love, expressed in assent and adherence to the Divine Lover in the only way currently possible?

Growth in this prayer costs dearly—in parched affections, impotence of reason, dull and dormant memory. A person who reaches out in response to a great calling, whether of genius or of grace, makes sacrifices that leave their marks of austerity upon personality. Says Jung:

> Great gifts are the fairest, and often the most dangerous, fruits on the tree of humanity... In most cases ... the gift develops in inverse ratio to the maturation of the personality as a whole, and often one has the impression that a creative personality grows at the expense of the human being.[13]

A paradigm of the cost to personality of turning from the world's values is found in the evangelical counsels. Poverty, celibacy and religious obedience limit development that normally prepares men and women for marital life, management of material things, and practice in decisions that radically determine their lives. The Second Vatican Council dealt with this trade-off: Paradoxically, the values renounced in pursuit of the evangelical counsels open the graced person to highly beneficial human development, of which Christ is the proof and model.[14] But to embrace the vows is to enter into jeopardy, and not all who enter come out on the high side. The same is true in the prayer of faith.

Personality develops wholesomely in intimate personal relationships and, in the prayer of faith, that relationship is with God the Father, in the Son, through the Holy Spirit. The disparity between the human and divine persons is here bridged through a wrenching transformation. It calls for David's attitude: "Though my flesh and my heart waste away, God is the rock of my heart and my portion forever" (Ps. 76:26). God-centered personality development does not always proceed in ways readily recognized or stamped with the world's approval, but proceed it does.

To summarize: In the prayer of faith, intellect is honed to develop acquired contemplation. Will is exercised in an ordeal of renunciation that beggars the training of athletes. Emotions, imagination and reason achieve new heights of integration with and submission to one's spiritual center, and become quiescent. Intellect is trained on God in faith, and will clings to God in an ever-growing attunement to the divine will. Ideally, the two wills function as one. A wayfarer now becomes a companion of God, cooperating with God to fulfill the divine plan for this world.

Personality Development in the Prayer of the Cloud

More remains to be said about the prayer of faith. In the older tradition, the prayer of simplicity was looked on as covering the whole ground between the prayer of affection and the prayer of quiet—the first stage of mystical prayer. But so different is the beginning from the end of the prayer of simplicity that two of the great mystical writers, Bossuet and de Caussade, treated the latter phase as a separate stage. They call that latter stage the prayer of faith. We follow their helpful division.

Even distinguished from the prayer of simplicity, the prayer of faith covers a vast range of growth. As we have seen, it begins with a dry effort in faith to dwell with God, and proceeds to an ever purer form of acquired contemplation. Thoughts, reflections, concerns, and distractions recede more and more into the background of consciousness during prayer, and even our self-awareness drops at times into a "cloud of forgetting" as we concentrate on the God of faith. Prayer becomes increasingly "a prayer of simple regard," a "prayer of loving attention."

If pilgrims stand firm in this hard prayer, which in its more intense forms is an experience of the dark night of the senses, they pass into a no-man's land between acquired and mystical contemplation (In acquired contemplation, our loving gaze is directed toward God in pure faith; in mystical contemplation, our loving gaze is an intuition, an inner sense of God's loving presence. This sense of presence results from divine, not human, activity.) When God acts in prayer, our self-actuation subsides. Thus, in the experience here described, our prayer becomes an amalgam of active and passive elements, and is neither the one nor the other with any clarity. As treatises like Belorgey's *Practice of Mental Prayer* make evident, this kind of prayer, leavened with mystical elements, ranges into a borderland between stages of prayer—a borderland unattainable by acquired contemplation, yet not possessing all the characteristics that would definitively entitle it to the designation, mystical contemplation.

A clarification: When prayer is called self-actuated, the term is not intended to deny that grace is at work, but only to affirm that the human experience is one of self-actuation. In mystical experience, on the contrary, the experience is one of passive receiving, much as we see the light of day without effort, and cannot prevent this seeing as long as we have sight and remain in the light.

Faced with this vast range and changing nature of the prayer of faith, can we do anything to improve our understanding? Would not another division be helpful? When we make a long arduous journey, we tend to divide it into stages according to the modes of travel: We travel by foot, by car, by ship, by plane. Analogously, we can clarify the prayer of faith by separating *the former from the latter reaches*. The latter reaches, which are assisted by divine transport, we christen *the prayer of the cloud*. A fourteenth century anonymous classic, *The Cloud of Unknowing*, seems to make this precision. The author named his book after the advanced phase of this stage of prayer which Bossuet only much later entitled *the prayer of faith*. Certainly, there is good reason for considering this advanced phase of the prayer of faith as a stage of its own, as it is distinguished by the first glimmerings of mystical prayer. St. John of the Cross, that master of mystical prayer, confirms the fact that mystical graces begin before the prayer of quiet, in the dark night of the senses.

The prayer of the cloud, the advanced phase of the prayer of faith, is one of the strangest stages of all, an almost-unanalyzable amalgam of what precedes, and what follows—the mystical prayer of quiet. The prayer of the cloud is composed of self-actuated prayer with low-level infusions of mysticism. It is non-mystical prayer with mystical elements, with the first blushes of the prayer of quiet. Too similar to the prayer of faith to be felt as a new call, it is only felt as a new experience.

The importance of the prayer of faith and the prayer of the cloud deserves highlighting. Many devoted pilgrims spend much of their prayer life in these two stages, never proceeding further. Some go beyond them, then return and remain in them, and never leave these stages again. Others return and then go on again. So these phases of prayer deserve our best attention.

Pilgrims arriving at the border of the prayer of the cloud have been wearily traversing the arid desert and foothills of the prayer of faith, struggling to dispose of distractions and unwanted preoccupations and to dwell with God. Now, as they top a hill, they find looming up an unassailable mountain of desolation: Acts of faith in God's presence seem unproductive and meaningless. Stubbornly standing at the base of this soaring cliff, they search out a handhold here, a toehold there. As the weeks and months pass, success! They are on the way up, advancing into the prayer of the cloud.

Clearly, the name is very apt. As they rise up the mountain of contemplation, mist and fog and clouds close in. In the prayer of faith, the mist obscured the eyes of the imagination. Here, the cloud penetrates the very command center of human knowing powers, shrouding it with darkness and, at times, even affecting it with a creeping paralysis.

What is this new mystery of growth? *The Cloud of Unknowing* puts it well: In this prayer of the cloud, pilgrims work to thrust everything that comes into their minds into the cloud of forgetting, as they stare in a kind of unseeing into the cloud of unknowing—staring blindly at God in pure faith. When anything—even self-awareness—comes to mind, it is thrust down into the cloud of forgetting. Such activity is within human competence, even if its deeper origin is divine. What urges pilgrims bravely on into the troubling unknown are the infused virtues of faith and love.

After long practice in pressing all that is not God into the cloud of forgetting, pilgrims enter more and more into the cloud of unknowing, passing into a domain that is ineffable, apophatic, beyond every resource of the mind to conceptualize or intellectualize or intuit. "The Lord intends to dwell in the dark cloud" (1 Kgs. 8:12).

To understand this better, let us draw a comparison. Human beings come to know one another by the help of images and concepts which our knowing powers produce with the help of the senses. No image or concept, however, can ever give us knowledge of God as he is. In heaven we will know God as he is because there he unites himself directly to our knowing powers. God takes the place of our self-produced concepts. Perhaps the best way to grasp that is to ponder the way we know someone whom we are embracing. At the level of the senses, it is a person-to-person contact without intermediary. In heaven, a like event will take place between us and God at the level of the spirit. It is already taking place between God and Mary and all the saints in heaven. It is the only way God can be known as he is.

A mystical touch of communion with God anticipates heavenly experience in a faint way. When the touch passes, the experience cannot be retained by created concepts. It is greater than they are. That is the problem here.

The role of pilgrims is to continue to thrust everything the mind conceives down into the cloud of forgetting; the role of God is to help them to pierce the cloud of unknowing. That help is not given in this stage except in vague and almost indiscernible ways identified only as this cloud of unknowing—or as fleeting mystical glimpses through the cloud. The doctrine here is expressed by St Denis: In this life, "The most godly knowing of God is that which is known by unknowing." Pilgrims may never know that they are being aided by mystical graces, so intangible are such graces in this stage.

Pilgrims may, however, experience *ligature*. It is an influence of the cloud of unknowing on the powers of knowing. Under this influence, pilgrims who try to think or remember or use words to pray meet with resistance, the way our bodies meet resistance when we walk through water, or the way our hand meets it when we try to lift an iron bar from a table beneath which a magnet is concealed. The magnet is God. God has been engaging the soul unawares in a low level of mystical prayer. Pilgrims are not conscious of this engagement until they try to say vocal prayers, examine their conscience, or read the office. Then they discover that their faculties go in slow motion, as through spiritual molasses. The cause is not interference with the powers of the soul, but their absorption, unawares, in the Presence, without any action initiated by themselves. St. Ignatius was at times so affected by ligature that he could spend the day trying to say the divine office.

At other times, pilgrims may return to themselves aware that for brief moments they have been *missing persons*—missing from themselves, utterly stripped of self-awareness, completely immersed, for minutes at a time, in the cloud of forgetting, by absorption in the cloud of unknowing.

What growth can the stage of the cloud of unknowing stimulate? Let us examine the change in comportment it is capable of inspiring, and then the interior change which produces it. *The Cloud of Unknowing*, chapter 54, waxes eloquent on the topic: Pilgrims in this stage develop a new facility to make themselves agreeable to persons low or high; they manifest such high spirits and wisdom and strength of presence that others seek out their company, and find joy, pleasure and help from it. On the other hand, persons who feign this prayer or delude themselves that they experience it are exposed by their simpering conduct—their pious, piping little voices, and their gestures of piosity.

The interior growth that underlies the change in comportment is summarized by the author of the *Cloud* in one word: This prayer "meeks" a person. The "meeking" comes about in this way: In laboring to thrust all into the cloud of forgetting and enter the cloud of unknowing, we discover that we ourselves are the most intractable obstacle. We may at times thrust everything else into the cloud of forgetting, but almost never ourselves. And we learn why. Sin in us is the obstacle. And so wide and so stubborn is our sinfulness that we begin to see ourselves as "a lump of sin."

More than all former meditations and tears, this experience plunges us into bottomless sorrow and generates a pure meekness and humility. Like a bad child on a journey with its father, we have no resources of our own, do not know the way, and are besides, the chief obstacle to going the way. How can we help but grow humble as we come into the presence of the Everything only to discover not only that we are "nothing," but are a negative nothing—are sin? As love made the Everything empty himself, take the "form of a slave" and then go down to the "nothingness" of death for our sakes (Phil. 2:7 ff.), it is drawing us "nothings" to confess our poverty as the only path to union with the Everything. Active here is a growing infusion of the gift of understanding, and the gift of wisdom which is knowledge fused with fiery love. Knowing human knowledge is powerless to know God as he is, we would gladly forget everything to be made to know Everything. Far deeper than words can reach, the pilgrim is saying, "On the rock too high for me to reach, set me on high . . ." (Ps. 61:3).

But to understand the power of this self-wretchedness, we have to go deeper. In the table of contents of *The Cloud*, the author writes, "A Book of Contemplation . . . in the which a soul is oned with God." This is the Christian understanding of the meaning of contemplation. One of its signs is occasional loss of self-awareness which, if authentic, is absorption in God which "perfectly meeks" the soul for an instant. The experience of the "nothingness" of self encountering the All of God can be so shattering as to plunge a pilgrim into the dark night of the soul. In the prayer of the cloud, however, there is only a touch of the experience.

At last the purpose of blind staring faith is growing clear. It is not primarily an effort to see, any more than a staring blind person is trying to see. Such blind staring is a concentration on something within. Here the concentration is on love; here, the heart, not the eyes, gazes. The eye is satisfied by seeing, but the heart is satisfied only by union.

Where does prayer go from here? In a sense, nowhere. Human powers can take us no further; we have even gone beyond them, as has been indicated. Having climbed to whatever heights we could reach by the current amalgam of acquired contemplation and infused graces, we are marooned on a mountainside. Even the *call* to the next stage of evolution cannot emerge, as heretofore, from within, from our unfolding powers and non-mystical graces which further their own development. We are bipeds on the Himalayas, yearning for the stars, but with no means of getting there. We are stranded.

Personality Development in the Prayer of Quiet

The summons to the prayer of quiet comes from without, if it comes at all. It has the nature of a visitation, not a summons. It is sheer gift, sheer mystical prayer. Here at last we are concerned with "those supernatural acts or states which our own industry is powerless to produce, even in a low degree, even momentarily."[15]

Recall that a stage of prayer is named according to its predominant characteristic or activity. Mystical graces have been experienced obscurely before this, at least in the prayer of the cloud, but the prayer itself relied heavily on human efforts. In the prayer of quiet, the essential event that gives the prayer its quality and its name manifestly descends from above, without any personal effort at the time—though the new stage of prayer will require much effort as it progresses.

The progress and development so far traced are dispositions for the onset of the prayer of quiet, but provide our pilgrim with no "right" ever to reach it. If it is given to a pilgrim, the onset of the prayer of quiet is passive, mystical. The experience is marked with different intensities in different persons, but its basic character remains the same. A fundamental form of the experience will be presented first, and explained; then an example of its more replete form will be given.

Suddenly, surprisingly, unannounced, the pilgrim is visited. Where before there was one person present, now there are two. God's presence is *felt*. It involves no human effort to remember, evoke or call God. The Presence is unsummoned by any human action. Loneliness departs. There is a sense of sweet intimacy and closeness of God to the soul. The intellect does not directly participate in the experience by a vision of any kind—but is aware of the soul's experience of the Presence, an experience that has the same solidity and indubitability as sense experience, though it is not of the five senses.

It must be stressed that no human effort brought on this visit. It is not a result of human development, as in earlier stages. It had not been expected, nor is it assured as a sequel to what went before. It may not even come during prayer. More than any experience up to this point, it comes as a surprise. Before, transitions were a gradual process, and changes subtle and hardly adverted to, so that awareness of entering a new stage came by hindsight. There were no surprises. Now the event is a startling surprise. The hiker on the Himalayas has been met by One descending, met by God and lifted up to God. God is the traveler, God is the Visitor. His visit may last for a moment, or go on for hours and days.

One such visitation does not assure anyone of being established in the stage of the prayer of quiet. There must be repetition of the experience. How often? Graces vary with individuals, and we have no statistics. St. Teresa of Avila says of mystical graces that the Lord may not renew his gift for a year, or even for many years. Her conclusion is that we should not sit waiting like "blockheads," but return to other productive forms of prayer.

The prayer of quiet is named such for two reasons: It is the first stage in which prayer at times takes place while the pilgrim's powers of the soul are in repose; and in its more intense form, a deep sense of quiet suffuses the whole person, as will now be described.

Suddenly, another visitation. This time, the Name of the Visitor is Quiet. Quiet bathes the pilgrim, body and soul, feelings, affections, mind and will. Most people do not dream that Quiet is a Person, but that this is a personal visit the pilgrim cannot doubt. "It is the Lord!" (Jn. 28:8). It is a delightful surprise, because quiet is envisioned as an absence—of conflict, of upset, of noise. In this experience Quiet is the presence which gives this stage its name. It can be explained by the fact that the pilgrim is being blessed with a taste of the next stage of divine visitation, which is called the full union. In full union, all the spiritual powers of the soul are absorbed in the divine presence.

St. Augustine wrote that "Peace is the serenity of the soul, the tranquility of the mind, the simplicity of the heart, the bond of love and the union of charity." St. Thomas Aquinas defines peace as "the tranquility of order." The pilgrim has experienced all this as an effect of the divine presence and can now say that Peace is Someone.

One pilgrim reported to his spiritual director his "wonderful sense of peace—and something else, something I never experienced before—I *feel* God inside, my soul touches Him, like my hand on your desk; and even now the feeling does not stop."

"But how know for sure it is God?" someone may ask. The following rule of thumb can help to answer such a question. If there is a felt need to ask the question *at the time of the visitation*, the experience is not the prayer of quiet. God's coming in Quiet carries its own overwhelming certification, greater than any other proof possible. One who experiences it needs no proof. If a doubter asks the question, no more proof can be given than to the question, "How do you know you are you?" If a spiritual director asks it, it is too bluntly put. A pilgrim who has come this far is to be trusted to have such a deep knowledge of God that a case of mistaken identity can be ruled out at least provisionally. The question should be put by indirection, and if the gist of the response comes to, "I think it was God," it was not the prayer of quiet. Beyond that, time will tell. The presence of God will recur, and perhaps become almost habitual in some, though the first sense of Quiet may never be repeated. Added proof will come in the development of the pilgrim that follows, if the pilgrim lives up to the grace received. One further comment: Though a recipient of the grace will not doubt at the time of the experience, doubts can rise later, especially if planted by a spiritual director, or induced by a lack of knowledge about even the possibility of such graces.

Though the prayer of quiet is experienced as a discontinuity, in a deeper sense, it is not. The turnabout is only in the source of activity. Here, it can be said, God is the exercitant. In the prayer of faith, we reach God in faith. In Quiet, the Lord reaches us. In love we have found one another.

Spiritual theologians analyze this state as a union of wills. The heart has attained its desire. For the moment, the quest is over. That explains the quiet, the peace.

Union of the intellect, which is a visual experience in the interior, spiritual faculty of knowing, lies further along the way, in the prayer of full union.

In what way does personality develop in this stage? First, we will treat of the changes this stage produces, then of the explanation. St. Teresa, in her *Interior Castle*, Fourth Mansions, says that Quiet confirms our trust in God, increases our desire to please God, and to have fruition in God. It strengthens our faith that God will be with us, so that we lose our fear of trials and sufferings and loss of earthly goods. Coming to better know the greatness of God, we see the inconsequence of earthly things, detach ourselves from them, and become our own masters. We find ourselves strengthened in all the virtues, and feel sure we will continue to progress if only we don't turn back. St. Teresa cautions, however, that all these benefits do not come from one divine visitation. We must continue to receive the divine favor.

St. John of the Cross in *The Dark Night of the Soul*, says that the dark night of the senses begins in the prayer of quiet. In book one, chapters 12 and 13, he describes the advances produced by this first dark night. The soul is illumined to know the greatness of God, and its own wretchedness. It learns respect and courtesy toward God. Like Job, it sits on a dunghill, but this is the dunghill of its own sins and faults. It learns to love and esteems others whom it disdained before. So cast down is it, that it becomes submissive and eager for any guidance. God so restrains its concupiscence that it neither finds nor aspires to the ready pleasures of sense that before enslaved it. This aridity crushes and subdues its natural energy as well. In summary, it gains the delight of peace, the habitual remembrance of God, purity of soul, and the practice of many virtues. Despite all its sufferings, its inner self is at rest.

What produces this development is that the personality has made a great leap forward in its union of wills with God. That is, it has been given a privileged taste of God as love. It has leaped forward in love, which theologians call "the form of all the virtues." By this they mean that no virtue is completely developed unless love gives it its finished character, and integrates it into the whole personality. St. Paul teaches this doctrine where he says that without love, a person is nothing, no matter what he does, gives, or accomplishes. Love is the seedling of universal development. The new growth of love that has sprouted in this stage will continue to spring up through the years in both personality growth and service of the kingdom.

Here it is necessary to consider the science and art of the discernment of spirits (DS), for this union of wills with God must work itself out in daily life through DS. DS is an activity which permeates all the stages, but it has a natural affinity with the prayer of quiet. A "natural affinity" here means that DS fits hand-in-glove with the prayer of quiet, because that prayer enjoys a familiarity with God that is sorely needed to discern spirits. Without such familiarity, we can discern spirits no better than a cripple can walk. DS is an effort to learn God's will for us. The effort involves both activity and passivity (receptivity). Obviously, it would do no good to seek God's will unless he is revealing it, and we are attuned to his disclosures. The person who enjoys familiarity with God has an advantage because of being sensitive to God's communications.

DS can be defined as the spiritual process of learning God's will in Christ so we can make right decisions. The process involves these elements: learning and accepting the normative guidance of the teaching Church; giving proper weight to our state and circumstances in life; using common sense in gathering data that bears on the decision we are considering (as, for instance, to follow a certain vocation, pursue a certain career, or enter into a marriage); praying for the guidance of the Holy Spirit; and, finally, tuning in to our affectivity states. If we are not in the grip of inordinate passions and desires, they are capable of communicating to us both the Holy Spirit's guidance and will and our own truest and deepest aspirations.[16] DS can be used spontaneously and almost instantaneously to facilitate lesser daily decisions.

More broadly, mature DS is a habitual practice of reading and monitoring the impulses, moods, and motions of our affective states. This process is immensely promising for a happy and fruitful life. It enables expert discerners to learn, from shifts in consolation and desolation, when they are taking the right course or departing from it. It also helps them to weed and keep order in the garden of their affectivity.

Why are states of, and variations in, affectivity a guideline for discernment and decision making? Because they register, at the level of feeling, a felt rightness and harmony, or wrongness and disharmony, between our deepest selves, our decisions, and the guidance of the Holy Spirit ("For it seemed good to us and the Holy Spirit"—Acts 15:28). Understanding of this process is helped by knowing that *theological consolation* is defined as every increase of faith, hope and love of God and joy in divine things. *Theological desolation* is defined as the opposite: a sluggishness and sadness except in the pleasures earth has to offer. Right decisions produce consolation; wrong decisions plunge us into desolation.

Such shifts in feeling are reliably followed, however, only by one whose life of the senses has been weaned and purified of slavery to worldly pleasures. That is why those who have reached the prayer of quiet have such facility in discerning spirits. They recognize the true consolation that attends right decisions, and distinguish it from mere sense pleasure. Only the former seems good to an intellect formed in the faith of the Church, and to a will and affections cleansed by contact with God; and they recognize desolation—the sense of being errant and lost—that attends wrong decisions. Part of the process of learning DS, however, involves learning to distinguish theological desolation from depression, that common emotional illness. Because depression makes it difficult to discern spirits, major decisions should be postponed if possible when it prevails. The same can be said for desolation, which is not always caused by personal fault. When desolation prevails, we must redouble our efforts to pray and be faithful, and await the return of consolation.

We cannot expect that finding and doing God's will is going to bring consolation unless we have gone through a long process of purification. Only then does finding and yielding to God's will bring that happiness, peace, and tranquility of right order which suffuses the senses as well as the will. Only when our feelings have been cleansed by virtue and grace do they reliably register our spiritual "comfort level" as we consider a decision from the "command center" of our inmost being, and embrace or depart from some aspect of truth and our true way.

Consider habitually sinful persons: They can be thrown into what they consider desolation simply by thought of the burdens attached to certain decisions. And they can find sense-bound consolation in deciding on what is in fact mortal sin.

The prayer of quiet, then, facilitates discernment of spirits. Besides advancing union with the divine will, the experience of Quiet provides a rare and pure experience of theological consolation. Henceforth, the memory of it can be used to recognize genuine consolation, and to expose its fake counterparts, such as relief (from a burden we are declining, but perhaps should not), satisfaction (from a work we are accepting, but perhaps should decline), or euphoria (a natural or even neurotic feeling that all is very well, when it may not be). Natural relief, satisfaction, and euphoria may have nothing in common with an increase in theological faith, hope, and love.

Marked wisdom and skill in DS is perhaps the surest sign of spiritual and psychological maturation, because it both guides conduct wisely, and assures further growth by providing an effective means of dealing with errant thoughts, moods and conflicts.

Using DS to monitor inner life does not consist in crushing and repressing unwanted thoughts, feelings, impulses and moods. Rather, it acknowledges them as part of the self, whatever their initial source in or outside the self; it tries to understand and assess them; it determines which to cultivate and which to allow to wilt by withdrawing from them the sunlight of attention and volition, and calming fears and worries about them. When we learn to discountenance worries, fears, dreads and desires, and replace them with their contraries, we strip them of their tyranny. When the tree of love grows tall, the weeds in its shade die.

Some pilgrims practice DS intuitively, without any sophisticated knowledge of its details. One man, who is unacquainted with the doctrine on prayer here discussed, nonetheless manifests a Christian conduct and equanimity which are two of its best fruits. He describes his secret: "When dissatisfaction with life, depression, and other such moods move in, I say to Our Lady, 'Remember, O most gracious Virgin Mary, that never was it known . . .' Then I turn my attention to what is at hand, attend to it, and the other thing fades." His three-step method (appeal for divine aid, elective application, and selective attention) is a simplified use of the gist of the process of DS as it has just been described. But his method would be unworkable without strength of character. If we lack character, we must begin by developing it.

Complex in description, the actual process of discerning and moderating the inner life can be simple. Nature abhors a vacuum; weakness reigns only when strength is absent. Negative psychic conditions can do us the favor of alerting us to the positive conditions we have failed to cultivate. Once alerted, we may nurture growth, and call on the Lord who gives increase.

The full range of DS, however, is a subtle art and science difficult to master, even at the advanced stage of the prayer of quiet. As with any art or science, mastery requires that personal charism and experience be supplemented by all that expert guides and teachers have garnered from the Scriptures, Saints, and tradition of DS elaborated in the writings of those who have mastered DS. More dramatically: Just as the evolutionary development of a species is communicated biologically, the evolution of wisdom is communicated socially. Neither the one nor the other is attained without receiving something from the parent stock. The Holy Spirit did not dispense with human agency even in the case of Saul. Ananias was sent "to help you recover your sight and be filled with the Holy Spirit" (Acts 9:17).

Some closing comments may help to ward off misuse of this chapter. Its purpose is to illuminate the relationship between prayer and growth of personality. It is not detailed enough to give direction for conduct in any stage of prayer, nor is it meant to imply that, once put behind us, the practices in any stage are no longer useful. People who travel by plane do not thereafter cease to walk, run, swim, and if necessary, crawl. A baby can go by plane while he has still before him the task of learning these other modes of locomotion. The analogy applies to prayer. St. Teresa of Avila was given a taste of advanced prayer, then thrown back for years on the need to meditate with the help of books. This is not uncommon. Even when pilgrims develop along the classic lines presented, they must often fall back on earlier methods of prayer—including vocal prayer.

It is instructive to compare the doctrine of the anonymous *The Cloud of Unknowing* with the later, more developed doctrine of St. Teresa. She repeatedly cautions us not to sit like "blockheads," inactively awaiting the return of some mystic grace. She insists that we must continue praying often over the humanity of Jesus, especially in his passion, with the simple gaze of the imagination, as in the prayer of simplicity. Not only does she teach that such prayer is no obstacle to those in the most sublime states of prayer, but without it they will not reach the final heights of prayer (*Interior Castle*, Sixth Mansions, ch. 6 and 7).

Gifts of mystical prayer facilitate the growth of holiness and personality, but they are not the only way. Obdurate desire for them impedes both them and holiness. We would not be amiss to think that one Holy Communion is more exalted than any mystical grace.

The real question is, *How shall I conduct myself to accord with my present graces and stage of prayer?* Perhaps the best answer is: Learn as much of the doctrine of prayer as you can, but in the end, with the help of a spiritual director, follow your own heart.

For natives of this mysterious land of the spirit, less traveled stages of prayer and personality growth lie ahead. But this is as far as we shall go.

Notes

[1]*Webster's Ninth New Collegiate Dictionary*, "personality".

[2]Karl Rahner and H. Vorgrimler, *Theological Dictionary* (New York, Herder & Herder, 1965), article "Person."

[3]Rahner and Vorgrimler, article "Personality."

[4]See, for instance, Wilhelm Reich, *Character Analysis* (New York, Farrar, Strauss & Giroux, 1960), pp. 189-202.

[5]J. P. Chaplin, *Dictionary Of Psychology* (New York, Dell Publishing Co., 1975).

[6]Reich, pp. 145-162.

[7] Austin Flannery, *Vatican Council II* (Collegeville, The Liturgical Press, 1975), Dogmatic Constitution on the Church, # 33, p. 390.

[8] C. G. Jung, *Modern Man In Search Of A Soul* (New York, Harcourt, Brace & World, 1933), p. 39.

[9] Karen Horney, *Neurosis And Human Growth* (New York, W. W. Norton & Co., Inc., 1950), pp. 24, 111, 158.

[10] *Spiritual Exercises Of St. Ignatius*, ## 112, 114.

[11] St. John of the Cross, *Dark Night Of The Soul* (New York, Image Books, 1959), Book II, ch. 3, p. 96.

[12] Karl Stern, *The Third Revolution* (Harcourt, Brace & Co., 1954), p. 244.

[13] C. G. Jung, *The Development Of Personality*, in *Collected Works*, vol. 17 (New York, Pantheon Books, 1954), p. 141.

[14] Austin Flannery, op. cit., Pastoral Constitution on the Church in the Modern World, # 45.

[15] R. P. Poulain, *The Graces Of Interior Prayer* (St. Louis, B. Herder & Co., 1911), p. 1.

[16] For a fuller treatment of DS, see the author's *The Pilgrim Contemplative*, (Collegeville, MN, The Liturgical Press, 1977).

Chapter Three

A Method for Eliminating Method in Prayer

Mental prayer is, or should be, one of the most personal of all activities. It is an interpersonal activity involving mutual love and self-communication, and nothing is more personal than loving.

Still, beginners in mental prayer usually need helpful hints drawn from the lives of the saints and others proficient in prayer. These helpful hints come down, in practice, to a method of prayer.

Here is a genuine dilemma. A method is an invasion of prayer; a lack of method means inability to pray. How do we solve the dilemma? *By giving beginners a method of prayer together with insistence that they jettison the method as soon as they can proceed without it.*

Among another class of meditators an even more serious dilemma arises. These are the people who have made progress in prayer and withdrawn from method for awhile, only to find now that their spontaneous prayer has grown sterile. They seem to need method once again, only now the happy remembrance of personalized prayer induces such a revulsion for method that they are tempted simply to drift rather than submit to codified guidelines again.

It is above all to the people in the second dilemma that I propose a method for eliminating method in prayer. What these people really need is a method of preparing themselves for prayer. *They need a method outside of prayer for eliminating method in prayer.*

This method for eliminating method is, therefore, not for beginners. It presupposes one experienced in prayer. The method for eliminating method contains, incidentally and subordinately, a method to be used *in prayer* in emergencies. This contingency use will be explained later.

It is my conviction that virtually all who pray mentally need some method of preparing for prayer if they want optimal prayer and progress in prayer. For this reason I recommend the method of eliminating method even to those who are not conscious of either of the dilemmas presented above. The preparation for prayer to be proposed here can be used as a method for eliminating method above all by those who have reached the prayer of faith or even gone beyond it. As a preparation for prayer which *can be* taken into prayer, the process to be described will be as salutary for beginners in prayer as for anyone.

Preparation for Prayer

The best time to make preparation for the next day's mental prayer is in the evening before retiring. This is true even if the mental prayer is not to take place in the morning. The reason for this insistence on the night preparation is the nature of the human psyche. Human thought profits by an incubation period in which to germinate or gestate. We are inclined to the idea that all of our thinking is done consciously, but the fact is, as Freud noted, that conscious psychic activity is only the latest arrival on the scene of psychic life. The soul never sleeps, and the night can be used to good purpose by collecting oneself to God before retiring. God "gives to his beloved in sleep" (Ps. 127:2). Pre-retirement recollection is important even in the shape it gives our dreams. Furthermore, preparation for prayer gives our thoughts a definite focus that feeds both our conscious and subliminal psychic processes during the day. Many great breakthroughs in human thought have flashed into consciousness at moments when the subject of the insight was giving all conscious attention to some other affair. This is proof enough that the inner life of human beings goes about the concerns of the heart even when they are least aware of it. These gifts from the inner life, however, are not altogether gratuitous. We must plant our questions and our hopes consciously if we want our subconscious to give the increase. We do just that by making evening preparation for the next day's mental prayer.

Once we become proficient at making this preparation for mental prayer, it need take but a few minutes. Initially, though, ten or fifteen minutes are required.

An ideal way to begin the preparation is to read a brief passage from the Gospels, lay the Gospels aside, and ask oneself the critical question: *What do I want to meditate about?* At stake here is the insistent fact that prayer ought to begin *with oneself.* A brief reading from the Gospels can establish the climate of prayer, but only the person involved can specify the optimal starting point. To automatically meditate on the passage just read can be a fatal error for the next day's meditation. Of course, if one wants to take up the Gospels and make them the subject of meditation, one should do it, because in that case one is in reality starting with one's felt desire here and now.

In prayer I must begin with myself. I am the only apt launching platform for my prayer. The reason is that prayer, as has already been said, is one of the most personal of all activities. To start with something other than self is to invite the meditation to become a study rather than a prayer. No one who wrote a book of meditation points months or years ago can tell me here and now what I want to meditate about. Here and now the points probably would not be apt for the author! Those who use point books ought to use them as I suggest they use the Gospels. Read a set of points, lay the book aside, and ask: *Now what do I want to meditate about?* If the answer is: *The points I have just read*, do not use them exactly as they are, but personalize them according to the method which will be introduced shortly.

If it can be said as a general truth that the failure to pray suggests a failure in the love of God, it can also be said that failure to pray personally enough signals the failure to love rightly. Accordingly, we seek to discover apt and personal prayer each day.

Apt and personal prayer can only start with myself, as I am here and now, this day, this evening, with its whole train of circumstances, concerns and desires. If I ignore the whole existential situation, and let a book impose a prayer subject upon me according to such a random determinant as the page I happen to be on, my prayer cannot possibly emanate from that personal psychic center where my in-depth living is going on. Neither my heart nor my attention will be captured by such prayer. I will remain divided between my concerns and my prayer.

Approaching the same point from another avenue, we can say that there is no really deep prayer without recollection, and there is no recollection without presence to the self. I must be collected to myself and my deepest concerns before I can communicate myself to God or to any other. Only if we enter those inner depths of the self where what we really are, unknown to others and often even to ourselves, is operative, can we enter into profound relationships with the Eternal I-AM. Profound relationships depend on self-communication. If we do not here and now possess the self, how can we communicate it? We've all had dinner with persons so distracted by every trivial occurrence in the room that they were no companions at all. Their hollow presence was an insult. This comparison is an apt one. Even the Lord likens prayer to an intimate meal together: "Behold, I stand at the door and knock. If anyone hears my voice and opens the door, I will enter his house and dine with him, and he with me" (Rev. 3:20).

I must, then, choose my focus and make my points out of my own reality to release my own love. That is, I must do this unless lack of prayer experience, exhaustion, or utter dryness compels me to go for help to another. When that happens, I must return as soon as possible to my own initiative. My own points may not sound as sublime or be as sublime as those in books, but they may stir my emotions, insights, convictions, and actions much more powerfully.

We must bring our current hopes, expectations, frustrations, concerns, and desires into our preparation. Please note: I am *not* saying: "Make your problems your prayer; bring your problems into your prayer." Such advice would in no way constitute a method for eliminating method in prayer. I *am* saying: Do bring your problems into your *preparation* for prayer so that, if it is not necessary, you will *not* have to drag them into your prayer. In your preparation, begin with your current concerns; and within the few minutes it takes to prepare points, you will often see that they are really trivial matters yapping at your heels and demanding of you an outsize amount of concern and worry. By giving them your sharp attention for a moment, you can "spank them and put them to bed," and then go far beyond them to give your freed attention to the realest, deepest concerns of your inner self. Only in this way are you likely to have the undivided attention absolutely necessary to pursue your real desire, which, in advanced prayer, is to find the Beloved.

There are times when our preparation will begin with a current problem and end with a current problem. Fine! If that is the case, we have discovered that the concern is grave enough to require prayer. We can now make our concern our prayer, instead of letting it nag us in prayer, as it certainly would if even our full attention cannot lay it to rest. Many worries and concerns wear away both us and our prayer only because we never clearly and definitively focused on them, resolved to do what we can about them, and then committed them to God.

This sensible approach will gradually eliminate our parasitic worries and put all our concerns into proper perspective. When the surface calms, we look into our depths and see our truest needs, longings and desires. Then and only then can we make them the part of our prayer and our lives that they deserve to be. We have triumphed over the distractions, decoys, and red herrings. We are on the way to finding our true selves.

Finding and Facing Self

It is difficult to find ourselves, especially in the beginning. It takes courage to seek out what we are. It takes industry to reject the laziness of rote. It takes energy to think and probe. None of us want to use method, but laziness or insecurity can make it necessary. Yet it is only by entering deeply, personally, subjectively into prayer, and engaging in a genuine personal relationship with Jesus, that we can avoid reducing prayer to a mere surface phenomenon incapable of producing fire in mind and heart, and so incapable of catalyzing that inner renewal which the Gospels call *metanoia*. The psychiatrist C. G. Jung addresses this very Christian issue:

> The demand made by *Imitatio Christi*, i.e., to follow the ideal and seek to become like it, should have the result of developing and exulting the inner man. In actual fact, however, the ideal has been turned by superficial and mechanical-minded believers into an

object of worship external to them, an outward show which, precisely because of the veneration accorded it, cannot reach down into the depths of the psyche and transform it into a wholeness harmonizing with that ideal. Accordingly, the divine mediator stands outside as an image, while man remains fragmentary and untouched in the deepest part of him. Christ can indeed be imitated to the point of stigmatization without the imitator's even remotely approaching the ideal or heeding its meaning; the point here is not a mere imitation that leaves a man unchanged and makes him into an artifact—it is rather a matter of realizing the ideal on one's own account *(Deo concedente)* in the sphere of one's individual life.[1]

Cowards who fear entering into themselves or into Christ will never make maximum progress in prayer or salvation: "But the legacy for cowards . . . is the second death in the lake of sulphur" (Rev. 21:8). Of course, those who have troublesome psychological problems must, in prudence, avoid entering those areas of the self which are dangerous territory. For them, God will provide.

It is much easier to follow someone else's thought pattern than to plough my own way into the future through the use of my own personality, initiative, and effort to think. It is much easier to use someone else's points for meditation than to generate my own. But, in many matters, unless I choose my own subject for meditation and formulate my own points, I will journey, not in my own direction, but in that of others. I will enter into their thoughts, not mine. I will enter into their self-discoveries, and perhaps never discover myself. When we want objective truth, we must go to the Church and to all who are wise. But in matters of legitimate personal concerns and paths to happiness, there is no substitute for one's own inner voice. The book of Sirach has some telling words on the point:

> Finally, stick to the advice your own heart gives you,
> no one can be truer to you than that;
> since a man's own soul often forewarns him better
> than seven watchmen perched on a watchtower.
> And besides all this beg the Most High
> to guide your steps in the truth.
>
> *Sirach 37:13, 17, 14, 18*

Unlike extrinsic assistance, self-made points hold real promise of self-transformation. When we make our own points we are most likely to find the way down into our inner depths and unleash the white hot magma of love and desire that will then break forth into the conscious world of affection and action for Christ. One is best able oneself to find and tap one's own potential energies.

The thought that goes into making points constitutes a kind of discovery that is true personal experience, and there is no substitute for it. I must begin with what are really *my* questions and *my* yearnings if the answers experienced are to move me deeply enough to change me into the likeness of Christ. No one else can experience for me, and no one can fully communicate to me his experience. Let Jung address himself to this felt need for one's own experience of profound realities:

> The best cannot be told... and the second best does not strike home. One must be able to let things happen. I have learned from the East what is meant by the phrase *Wu wei*: namely, "not doing, letting be," which is quite different from doing nothing. Some Occidentals, also, have known what this not-doing means; for instance, Meister Eckhart, who speaks of *sich lassen*, "To let oneself be." The region of darkness into which one falls is not empty; it is the "lavishing mother" of Lao-tzu, the "images" and the "seed." When the surface has been cleared, things can grow out of the depths. People

always suppose they have lost their way when they come up against the depths of experience. But if they do not know how to go on, the only answer, the only advice that makes any sense is "Wait for what the unconscious has to say about the situation." A way is only *the* way when one finds it and follows it oneself. There is no general prescription for "how one should do it."[2]

There is still another compelling reason for us to make our own points. Unless we do we may fail not only to open a fissure through which the flaming energies of our inner life can emerge to become the vital force of our prayer; we may fail to open our inner life deliberately and consciously to God, and to ourselves in God's presence, so that we can deal with the contingencies this self-knowledge gives rise to, and expose the paleness and sickness we will find there to the healing light and care of God. We are afraid and ashamed to expose ourselves even to God, though God alone can heal us. We are also afraid to discover God in our own depths for fear of the divine claims of love and mandate for change that will result. Jung has clearly discerned the widespread fear of these inner realities, and found it in high places where it ought not exist:

If the theologian really believes in the almighty power of God on one hand and in the validity of dogma on the other, why then does he not trust God to speak in the soul? Why this fear of psychology? Or is, in complete contradiction to dogma, the soul itself a hell from which only demons gibber? Even if this were really so it would not be any the less convincing; for as we all know, the horrified perception of the reality of evil has led to at least as many conversions as the experience of good.[3]

How can we make full progress in prayer until we expose our inner life naked to both God and ourselves? How become fully human unless we admit that the furnace of our psychic life burns with the raw energies that can be fashioned into every human desire and every exalted and perverted action that has ever come out of a human being? How be fully human without knowing what we can become, and asking God to help us avoid what we might become and become what we ought? Without self-knowledge, how be deep, or fully unified, or recollected, or ourselves? How face reality, or communicate ourselves whole and entire to God and one another?

It is clear to a student of comparative religions like Professor Mircea Eliade that human beings both love and fear God. We want to run to God and run away. Our psychic life is an amorphous, many-valenced thing. Subconscious currents run in contrary directions. We can both love and hate God, cherish and resent God. Leonard Bernstein's symphony *Kaddish* vividly portrays this maelstrom of emotions which we hide in the subconscious because we think it would be blasphemous to let it break through and surge into the open daylight of consciousness. Yet where else can it be tamed and channeled? Where but in daylight and the open air of exposure to God's grace can it cool and harden and thereafter remain, like the granite and the basalt of the earth, as the memory of the ancient volcano of our revolt, and of God's understanding forgiveness and loving conquest over the self-destructive contradictions rending our inner selves?

There are nuns who need a psychiatrist to tell them they would like to have children; there are nuns and priests who leave the religious life when they discover they have desires for marriage. These people have lived a life divorced from their own souls. Every healthy nun knows she would like a husband and children, and every normal priest knows he would like to marry. That is, they know they share with every human nature these intense longings and powerful drives. No priest or nun is called to suppress these longings by trying to pretend they do not exist. They are rather called to control these drives and consciously forego the joy of their fulfillment for the sake of pursuing their higher, virginal love of Christ and the Church.

The practice of daily communing with our deepest selves to prepare for meditation will help us to keep posted on all these powerful and dangerous currents within us. Suppression of awareness permits dangerous psychic pressures to mount, while these vents into consciousness will have the opposite effect. The foul gases of cold or hateful or resentful feelings toward God can escape, giving us opportunity to feel ashamed, apologize, and be cleansed and healed.

A few weeks of practice should enable experienced meditators to make their own points without difficulty. Once they have discovered the benefits, they will continue. These confident statements presuppose that the persons addressed are doing daily spiritual reading, especially of the Scriptures. They presuppose a broad knowledge of Scripture and the memory of hundreds of favorite passages which come to mind spontaneously when they are germane to the thoughts of the meditation. Those who lack a familiarity with Scripture may find the method impossible. Healthy Christian prayer seems hardly sustainable without the knowledge or use of Scripture, wherein God teaches us to pray.

Only two people know what I ought to pray about here and now: God and myself. In fact, I reduce that to one. God knows, and I must find out. That is the task for each night. By starting with myself I am most likely to be able to find out. I do it by making points. It is also there, in my deepest recesses, that I am most likely to find God. And only if I find Him will I be truly at prayer, which is not thinking, but communication and communion. Prayer is a work of two.

Making Points

We come now to consider the actual making of points. As I set about the task, I should be consciously guided by two master facts. The first is the stage of prayer I have reached, and the second is my frame of mind at the moment. Often these two concerns are in conflict, and the points must resolve the conflict.

> *Master fact one:* Our state of prayer guides us. In slightly advanced states of prayer we are commonly ruled by the desire to find God in prayer. We no longer want to reflect on spiritual truths or current events in our lives. We want God's company. Furthermore, we are plagued by a loss of the ability to meditate. The reasons for this are explicated in chapter one, and are elaborated in many treatises on prayer.

> *Master fact two:* Our mental and emotional state must guide the way of prayer. For instance, we may be troubled by an event of the day, and want to pray over it.

These two desires are in conflict. Unless we resolve the conflict before trying to meditate, we are likely to drift back and forth between the two concerns, not knowing which is the prayer and which the distraction.

I would like to give an example of a set of points made in this state of conflict. I am in a stage of prayer in which I habitually want to find God. At the same time I am concerned about my health. Apparently I have done what I can for it, but concern remains. During the last two or three days, the worry has introduced itself into my prayer.

For the Subject of Meditation I choose:*The Divine Physician.* The Scene to occupy my imagination: *Jesus putting clay on the blind man's eyes.* The Grace I ask: *To put myself in the care of the Divine Physician.* I now think about the subject for a moment (instinctively guided by the two master facts listed above), and reflectively expand it into three points:

First point: The God-man, the true Physician.

Second point: I put myself completely in Your care, Divine Healer.

Third point: Lord, now that I am Your concern, You can be my concern.

I now choose a phrase which in a few words captures the essence of the meditation. I call it the *Spiritual capsule: Divine Physician, abide with me.*

Something significant has transpired here. This simple preparation, taking only a few minutes, was actually a miniature meditation. In this preparation-meditation I have ended my concern by consciously turning it over to Christ. I eliminated the conflict and became free to pursue my heart's desire. That fact is crystalized in the third point, where my attention focuses on the Lord, and I actually begin my interchange of affection with him.

In this mini-meditation I have disposed myself for the prayer of the presence of God by giving my current concern the momentary attention it needed, which was all the attention it deserved. This telescoping of a meditation that might formerly have consumed an hour into a minute or two is characteristic of more contemplative states of prayer. It proceeds intuitively and almost instantaneously. It is also characteristic of contemplative states of prayer that meditation is displaced from prayer time and skillfully and spontaneously carried on at apt moments during the day, and during preparation for prayer. Prayer preparation is, in contemplative states, a time to run quickly through meditative matters, and thus dispose ourselves for peaceful contemplation.

Let us now take the example of a set of points which we might make if we are in the stage of the prayer of faith, on a quiet day when nothing is troubling us. The master fact governing our choice is our yearning for non-verbal communication with God:

Subject: Resting with You in faith.

Scene: Desert, where you took the Apostles to rest. (Mk. 6:31).

Grace: To be still and know that You are God. (Ps. 46:10).

First point: "Commune with your hearts on your beds and be silent" (Ps. 4:4).

Second point: "Peace, be still!" (Mk. 4:39).

Third point: "You lead me beside still waters, You restore my soul." (Ps. 23:3).

Spiritual capsule: God

There are a number of useful things to be noted in this example. We are addressing God even in the course of preparing points. We see no sense in talking about God in third person when we can address God directly. Further, we love to address God (and have God address us) in God's own words, so we have culled from Scripture passages recently memorized in the course of our Scriptural reading. We memorized them because they aptly describe and Scripturally vouch for the authenticity of our current form of prayer. Finally, we summarize our whole meditation in

one word, because contemplative prayer tends to the use of
as few words as possible.

When in the prayer of faith or beyond, we may frequently make points similar to this for months at a time—
or even years. We make fresh points each day to express
the nuance of the moment, but generally the essence
remains unvarying. We are in communion with God on a
deep level little affected by the transient times and tides of
each day.

The two examples given also illustrate a standard
framework, a Spiritual Filing Cabinet, to contain the
meditation. It is the format made familiar by Saint Ignatius. Its advantage is that of any filing cabinet. It facilitates
sorting my thoughts, filing them, and memorizing my
preparation for prayer. I never vary the cabinet but only the
contents. I write the meditation each night and, just before
falling asleep, easily recall it from memory. On evenings
when the preparation is fully successful, I will have disposed of all other concerns by the time I reach the third
point, and there be swept up into the presence of God,
where I hope to remain until after the hour of prayer the
next morning. In that case, I do not recall the points when
I compose myself for sleep. The points have eliminated
themselves by projecting me beyond them. *They have
proved their power to be self-eliminating.*

Let us exemplify a third mood, a composite of the two
preceding moods, and see the points that come out of it. We
are drawn to spend our prayer time simply dwelling with
God, but feel we ought to bring concern for the world into
our meditation. To which of these conflicting desires are
we really being called by grace? If we are in a contemplative stage of prayer such as the prayer of faith, the presump-
tion must be in its favor until experience gives contrary
evidence. After all, arrival at such a prayer is a personal
invitation from God to *come apart in prayer and rest*

awhile. Furthermore, by contemplation we are being fashioned into God's servant to the world. Still, in preparing our meditation, we may be able to harmonize the two diverse thrusts of our inclination.

Subject: The God of concern for the world.

Scene: The God of the world is in me, who am part of the world.

Grace: To be one with You laboring for all, my God and theirs.

First point: O God of all origins, Father ingenerate!

Second point: O God to the world, Incarnate God-Son!

Third point: O God to the world-being-reborn, Holy Spirit!

Spiritual Capsule: Come, O God-man!

In these points we gain a harmonic view of God and the world, thereby reconciling the seemingly opposed desires of our state of mind. Whatever direction our prayer takes in the morning, it is likely to proceed without the conflict of unreconciled contraries.

When time is available, it may be useful to jot down a few sub-ideas under one or more of the three points. Under the first point of the sample meditation just given, we might jot: "You are the father who has instructed us, 'Be fruitful and multiply; fill the earth and subdue it. Have dominion . . .'" Under the second we could add the words of Jesus: "Fear not, I have overcome the world," and "I have come that they may have life and have it more abundantly." Years ago, I used to find this helpful, but now I generally find it only clutters up the meditation and interferes with the simple contemplative gaze the preparation helps me to achieve.

Anyone willing to experiment with this method for eliminating method may discover with joy that the former wandering from one book to another in search of help for meditation has been replaced by rewarding self-consultation and divine consultation. "What do I want to pray about, Lord?" The answer comes readily: *The quiet of being with You.* "What scene to quiet my imagination?" *John leaning on Your heart.* "What grace?" *To renew my awareness of what it means to be with You.*

Point One: Resting here with You.

Point two: Listening in my heart to what You say.

Point Three: Returning the love.

Spiritual Capsule: I to you, and you to me, you whom my heart loves.

I have begun with something even more personal than Scripture. I have consulted God and myself, and from there gone on to selectively use Scripture as God's means of communicating with me and I with Him. Slowly I formulate where God and I are with one another now. I find God, and, as best I can, remain in God's presence until the time of formal prayer the next morning.

The Praying Itself

In the morning, I recollect myself the moment I awake. If, on awaking, I am in the presence of God, I make no attempt to recall my points. I simply remain with God. When I come to the formal time for prayer, I do not use my points. *Points are not for use.* I abide with God. I pray contemplatively, in a form of non-verbal communication represented by the names, *prayer of faith, prayer of quiet,* and so forth. Of course, this method does not produce such a state of prayer. It facilitates it for those who have attained it.

It is only by turning from thoughts of God that we can turn to God, for no thought can contain God, but a thought can distract us from God. One Sister to whom I had communicated these reflections wrote me: "I've read a little over half of *Ascent to Mount Carmel*. I like John. He is very gentle, thoughtful, and humble: 250 pages of how to do nothing in prayer. You said it in one sentence: 'Don't think about God, think God.' I understand that all this background is essential, though, especially since I have not yet learned how to do nothing."

This self-eliminating method can help us to bank the fires of our own recollection until it reaches the incandescence of the prayer of the presence of God. It is for those quiet enough to hear the call to this prayer, and courageous enough to take the solitary path to their meeting alone with God.

The points are designed for self-elimination, but they are also meant to serve as an emergency auxiliary. They help us to enter the orbit of our normal prayer, but they also rescue us if we fall out of it. Should I be unsuccessful in finding God when I awake in the morning, I recall my points and mentally run through them. I center my recollection around them until the time for formal prayer. On coming to prayer, I put aside my points and make another attempt to find God without thoughts or words. If I do not succeed, I resort to my points once again, since I have put into them the matters which mean most to me at the moment. They should help me to pray the prayer of simplicity, or the prayer of affection, or at least to do some meditating. If not, I will have to turn to some other alternative, such as meditative reading of the Scripture, but only as a good spiritual director, or reliable book on the stages of prayer, advises.

Sometimes when we attempt points we will find we are a void. We have no choice but to resort to a book. *Or do we?* That is the time to turn to *past sets of our own points*, prepared in richer seasons, and stored for barren days. At times when I have felt repelled by books and unable to prepare my own points, I have resorted to stores of my own points. Almost always two or three sets will guide me quickly into recollection and prayer. I experience again the grace I received in the day and hour I first used those points. Our past roads to God frequently remain viable if we can locate them again. We should return often to the sites where God has visited us in the past.

This method of preparing points is very useful even for those in earlier stages of prayer, but for them the preparation will not be self-eliminating. They will of necessity take the self-prepared material into the prayer and use it to feed the meditation. They will enjoy many of the benefits of this highly personalized and creative method of prayer. For them too it minimizes method, shuns impersonal elements, and guides to personal discovery of Christ.

The method needs some modification for beginners in prayer. They are not often able to prepare points out of their heads. It is preferable to take a Gospel event, analyze it, and put it into the spiritual filing cabinet according to their own bent. Under each point they should jot down personal ideas and experiences relating to the Scriptural theme. If no personal ideas come, they can be trained to use the references to related passages which most bibles provide. Looking up these related passages and jotting them down as sub-points will help deepen their understanding of Scripture and develop their power to meditate. Some fifteen minutes need to be invested in such preparation. Before long they will show more deftness and originality in use of the method.

A group of young Sisters were taught this method. Not long after, one of them wrote me: "At first when you told us about using our 'spiritual capsule' before bedtime and that in time we would awaken at night and find ourselves talking to God, I felt it would be years until that could ever happen to me. But it *has* happened!"

Post-Prayer Activity

After prayer, we should jot down beneath the points we used any worthwhile insights, experiences and meetings with God. It is like making deposits in a private spiritual bank account. As already indicated, reading them over some time later can be the best preparation for prayer. It is practicable to make points each day in a small note book, dating each day as we go along. Then we can easily return to some experience we may wish to ponder in the future.

This method for eliminating method in prayer has been well tested and proven. It requires some trouble on our part, but it eliminates a lot more trouble than it takes. It is a method with a high yield. For surely we who start not from some one else's starting point but from our own are likely to make the most progress in our journey to God.

Notes

[1] C. G. Jung, *Psychological Reflections*, ed. by Jolande Jacobi (New York, Harper Torchbooks, 1961), p. 279.
[2] Jung, p. 265.
[3] Jung, p. 322.

Chapter Four

Nature and Value of a Directed Retreat

During the last two decades the directed Ignatian retreat has been reborn. The directed retreat is a marked departure from the familiar preached retreat, in which we customarily spend some two hours a day hearing the word of God as it is spoken and interpreted by the retreat master.

The successful return of the directed retreat can in part be credited to that widespread phenomenon of our day, the passion for experimentation. The experimental approach springs from a twofold conviction: that we can produce something *better*; and that, in an age wherein proliferating options are overloading our decision-making powers, we must discover what is most *relevant*.

We have all benefited from the experimental approach. Consider agriculture. Twenty-five years ago there was widespread talk of the impossibility of feeding the world's people. Today there is not. That is largely because, in the interval, agricultural experimentation was carried on in the Philippines to produce a new strain of wheat. The first objective was to produce a *better* wheat, one that would give a greater yield per acre. The second objective was to produce a more *relevant* wheat, one hardy enough to flourish on poor land in cold climates. The result is IR-3. It revolutionized the growth of wheat, turning traditionally wheat-importing countries to wheat exporters.

In the field of religion, we have similar problems and similar inclinations. How raise up better Catholic Christians, people more in contact with God, more committed to

Him, more discerning of the will of God in a complex and confusing world, more faithful to the Church, more productive in the service of the Kingdom? How form more relevant Catholic Christians, people who can responsibly handle the increased responsibility laid on each today? Enterprising men and women in the Church have presented the directed Ignatian retreat as one answer.

Is it? I think it is, but my objective here is not to provide proof of that, but to give information concerning the nature of a directed retreat. Judgments can come later.

What is a directed retreat? I will proceed to answer that question by giving a series of progressively improving definitions until we reach the most illuminating definition I can provide.

Nature of a Directed Retreat

The directed retreat is a retreat made neither alone nor in a large group; furthermore, it is made without the help of several preached talks a day. This incomplete definition is meant to clarify the manner in which the directed retreat departs from the familiar preached retreat. The directed retreat involves one director and one retreatant operating in a one-to-one relationship. The director may or may not be directing other retreatants simultaneously, but in any case he or she guides each retreatant as though that person alone were on retreat. Of course, there may be some interplay between retreatants. They may celebrate Mass together. They may do shared prayer.

The directed retreat is a concerted effort to seek God in the smallest possible community. In a directed retreat, everything is set up and directed to help the retreatant *find God.* All irrelevant and distracting persons and entities are withdrawn. That leaves us with the smallest possible community, a community of three, in the likeness of the

Trinity. The community of three which results can be described in various ways. It can be seen as composed of the retreatant, God and the Holy Spirit; God is the goal, and the Holy Spirit is the agent. The Holy Spirit guides the retreatant to God, and is the Love between the retreatant and God. There is, from another viewpoint, the triad of the retreatant, the director, and the Holy Spirit. The retreatant and the director work out the retreat in concert, and the Holy Spirit is the one Guide of both. From a still more comprehensive viewpoint, the tripartite community is made up of the retreatant, God, and the Church (whom the director embodies and represents).

The reason for setting up this smallest-possible community is to promote the total personalization of the retreat. All transactions are aimed directly at the one retreatant's unique personal needs here and now. While it is true that God always can and does work as personally with an individual in a group as with an individual alone, the retreat director cannot. And conversely, the retreatant cannot. The fact that God can is the saving grace of group retreats. The fact that retreatant and director cannot is the reason there is at times no substitute for a directed retreat.

The tiny directed retreat community favors intimate contact that helps the retreatant come to know God and the Church in an intimate new way. By *intimacy* I mean an attentive, healthy, open and receptive relationship that is productive of a mutual identification in joys and sorrows.

The directed retreat is the engaging in spiritual exercises under the daily guidance of a director who has the twofold role of retreat director and spiritual director. The function of the retreatant is to do spiritual exercises. The function of the director is to guide and monitor the exercises.

In the directed retreat, there is emphasis on the activity of the *retreatant.* We have all seen the retreat master of the preached retreat deliver four and five talks a day, hear confessions, hold interviews, and stagger out of the house exhausted some days later. The directed retreat, on the contrary, demands much more of the retreatant, and focuses on what the retreatant is doing more than on what the director is saying. If the retreatant's activity still involves a great deal of active listening, it is not primarily to a human being but to God that the listening is attuned.

St. Ignatius repeatedly stresses the activity of the retreatant, who is called the *exercitant*. Ignatius introduces his little book for retreat as "*Spiritual Exercises* which have as their purpose the conquest of self and the regulation of one's life in such a way that no decision is made under the influence of any inordinate attachment" (#21).

The director gives the retreatant *daily* guidance. Generally, the two meet once a day. The director provides spoken or written points for meditation, and they are generally given very briefly. Directors with more than one retreatant may outline the points for meditation in common to save time, when this is not to the retreatants' disadvantage. It often is, since retreatants differ in the pace of finding the grace needed from each meditation to equip them for the next. To indiscriminately hand out the same material each day to a number of retreatants is to undermine one of the great values of the directed retreat. The director of a preached retreat is often aware that some on the retreat are not ready to proceed to the next stage of the retreat, but he is bound to present his material at a pace suited to the good of the majority. In the directed retreat, the director has the advantage of pacing the input to the needs of each, and to do otherwise is a serious mistake.

The retreatant gives the director a faithful account of the inner experiences and responses which took place in the course of his meditations, telling of joy or sadness, peace or unrest, hope or fear, attractions and repulsions.

This account of one's personal experiences is always given in a private interview. The account is at the heart of the directed retreat, as is the director's responding guidance. The practice of making this report develops the retreatant's ability to discern the movements of good and evil that play in the human mind, heart, and feelings. The guidance of the director helps retreatants learn how to distinguish between the good and evil influences more successfully. Most important, it helps them distinguish the Divine call from every other influence. This knowledge frees them from old slavery to whims and emotions and nagging feelings of guilt. It helps them put on the mind of Christ.

From what has just been said, it becomes manifest that directors have two clearly distinct functions. *First*, like the director of a preached retreat, they provide the retreatant with input for the meditations. Let it be added that, both in the brief way they provide this material (often in printed form) and in the selection of the material provided, they themselves are guided in a general way by their source material, *The Spiritual Exercises of Saint Ignatius*. Directors feed in this input in harmony with the retreatant's *actual accomplishments*, thus moderating the advance and flow of the retreat in a fully personalized way. Directors are aware that the graces sought in each meditation are necessary graces, which have to be built up in their proper order, like the parts of a building: Sorrow for sin is the excavation, forgiveness the foundation, knowledge of Christ the light along the path, etc. This careful control of the process of the retreat is certainly one of the great advantages of a directed retreat.

Second, the retreat director is the retreatant's spiritual director. The great religions of the world, even in their most mystical traditions, all teach the need of a guide, a guru, a starets, a roshi, a spiritual director. Without a director, there can be no making of the Spiritual Exercises in accord with the mind of St. Ignatius, as a reading of the Introductory Observations will establish. Without a director there has not been set up the necessary mini-community described in the second definition.

The director helps the retreatant to discern the mysteries of the interior life in a practical way that is meant to lead to practical decisions and practical service of Christ. The retreatant is always the primary discerner, and the director the auxiliary discerner. Only the retreatant is present to the pertinent inner experiences. Unless given an honest and faithful report, the auxiliary discerner cannot give the help he or she is meant to give.

The retreatant, then, is the subjective discerner. Directors are the objective discerners. As objective discerners, they interpret the experiences of the retreatant in accord with the biblical and doctrinal expressions of the revelation as it is guarded and developed and handed on by the whole Church. If the retreatants too are learned in theology, and sometimes even if they are not, they themselves may be able to interpret their experiences quite authentically. But in accord with the wisdom of the Church and of the revelation itself, the people of God do not rely on themselves individually, but depend on one another in the effort to understand, or at least confirm, the meaning of God's communications, even the individual and personal ones. If the retreatant is guided, presumably by the Holy Spirit, to come to a certain decision, directors can hope, by their knowledge of doctrine, the norms of the spiritual life, and the guidance of the same Holy Spirit, to confirm the decision.

The role of the director as auxiliary discerner is made even clearer if we consider the distinction between the role of the priest-confessor and the role of the *retreat spiritual director*. The Confessor in the sacrament of penance is concerned primarily with the moral order, with the person's conscious, sinful rebellion against God's will. The retreat spiritual director is concerned with the retreatant's inner experiences, moods, attractions and repulsions, even before the retreatant has made any deliberate free response to them. The Confessor wants to know what a person has done of good and evil. The director wants to know to what seeming good and what seeming evil the retreatant is being drawn through the inner experiences of prayer and meditation. St. Ignatius himself makes this distinction, and even specifies that the retreatant should feel free to go to a confessor other than the director:

> While the one who is giving the Exercises should not seek to investigate and know the private thoughts and sins of the exercitant, nevertheless, it will be helpful if the director is kept faithfully informed about the various disturbances and thoughts caused by the action of different spirits. This will enable the director to propose some spiritual exercises in accordance with the degree of progress made and suited and adapted to the needs of a soul disturbed in this way (#17).

It might be pointed out here that the director need not be a priest. He or she need only be a spiritually gifted person experienced in living the spiritual life, possessing the developed capacity to guide others, having a good knowledge of the faith, and knowing the *Spiritual Exercises* through exercise in them. This is a fact to be underscored, since if the one-to-one retreat is to proliferate, many directors will have to be drawn from religious men and women and other members of the laity. Numbers of Sisters and laymen are in fact now directing retreats.

Retreatants need openness and courage to give their directors the necessary account. Still, they do not need to steel themselves to bare their whole souls, as they sometimes find it necessary to do with their regular spiritual directors, and certainly find it necessary to do with their confessors.

A directed retreat is a retreat in which one is guided by a director to do spiritual exercises which will purge, illumine, and dispose one for direct communication and communion with God, direct guidance from God, and the readiness to do God's will. This final definition gives a comprehensive idea of the directed retreat. The Ignatian directed retreat is divided into four parts or *weeks*. It was Ignatius' hope that the retreatant would really spend a whole month, apart from all other business, in making the retreat. Thirty-day retreats are being conducted today. More often, however, the retreat is condensed and made in a period of six or eight days. The first *week* provides spiritual exercises of purgation. The second *week* provides spiritual exercises of illumination which call the retreatant to a more wholehearted commitment to Jesus. The third and fourth *weeks* invite one to share Jesus' experience of passion and resurrection as a preview of one's own future in Jesus' service and life. In everything, Christ is the retreatant's life, light, salvation, motivation.

Value of a Directed Retreat

The directed retreat is a search for *direct communication and communion with God.* To miss this would be to miss the meaning of the directed retreat. The preacher of the preached retreat is replaced not by the director, but by God. God personally hands on the message to the retreatant here and now. The retreatant hears God both in the words of Scripture and Catholic doctrine, and in the various inner impulses and movements of the passions which I have already identified as the experiences calling for discernment.

To come into a retreat with this expectation requires that both director and retreatant possess deep faith. No doubt this faith frequently falters in both, perhaps most when they are least aware of the fact. Some directors may not even have the conviction that this direct communication and communion with God take place, but then they are betraying their trust, for it is inescapably clear that this is the expectation and absolute conviction of the author of the *Exercises*, who writes:

> The director of the Exercises ought not to urge the exercitant more to poverty or any promise than to the contrary, nor to one state of life or way of living more than another. Outside the exercises, it is true, we may lawfully and meritoriously urge all who probably have the required fitness to choose continence, virginity, the religious life, and every form of religious perfection. But while one is engaged in the Spiritual Exercises, it is more suitable and much better that the Creator and Lord in person communicate Himself to the devout soul in quest of his divine will, that He inflame it with His love and praise, and dispose it for the way in which it could better serve God in the future (#15).

What Ignatius expects is that the retreatant will, by making the *Exercises*, repeat some of Ignatius' own experiences of God guiding him. Those experiences were so vivid that Ignatius called God his "Schoolmaster."

Let me point out here by way of example that we customarily describe the attraction to the priesthood or the religious life as a "vocation" or a "call" from God. St. Ignatius is simply broadening the base of that belief by affirming that God calls us directly to many things, every day, if we can hear God's voice, and if we will respond to it. God's call is experienced through the inner movements of love, joy, peace, attraction to a better way, etc. According to Fr. Karl Rahner, S.J., this is a case of grace breaking into consciousness. In essence, therefore, the directed retreat is meant to be a mystical retreat. It is a series of spiritual exercises and prayers and contemplations in search of the experience of God and the reading out of God's will. It is a transcendental relationship breaking into consciousness.

Directed *vs*. Preached Retreat

It should be of help to add a brief comparison of the directed and the preached retreat. The directed retreat is the authentic presentation of the *Spiritual Exercises*. This is a fact of history, but it also stands from an examination of the Introductory Observations in the *Spiritual Exercises*. Still, that does not mean that the directed retreat is always best for everyone, in every set of circumstances. St. Ignatius makes it clear in the Exercises themselves that not everyone is suited for them, or ready for them. Nor are they necessarily better for anyone, year after year. They have a certain inherent advantage, in that they guide the retreatant to listen directly to God. On the other hand, there are times when God sends us to human beings, as Paul was sent to Ananias after his conversion experience. Many factors must be weighed in determining which type of retreat will be best: the level of human maturity; the level of religious maturity; the personal needs at the moment, such as the need of making a decision concerning a state of life; the level of generosity, of restfulness, of vitality, etc.

The preached retreat remains of immense value when it is well conducted.

I support this simply by appeal to the years of experience many of us have had in making such retreats, and some of us in conducting them. Furthermore, preached retreats are excellent opportunities for hearing the word of

God, and human beings always remain bearers of that word. There is no substitute for the preached word of God, just as there is no substitute for the inner experience of God. Then too, preached retreats are an opportunity to share the personal faith vision and synthesis of retreat masters who can often communicate their faith-knowledge and experience with the help of some specialized theological, sociological, or psychological competence. A gifted and prayerful director not infrequently inspires some retreatants to enter as deeply, or even more deeply, into communication and communion with God as they would in a directed retreat.

What it comes to is that the preached and directed retreat are two species of retreats. Each has its own unique value, and each addresses itself to unique needs. The directed retreat is of unsurpassed worth for times when serious decisions have to be made. It is also of unsurpassed value in providing a guided and formative experience in living the interior life. It has immense value in helping a person find direct communication with God, and in coming to other primary religious experiences.

The preached retreat is especially valuable for broadening and articulating our knowledge and vision of faith. This helps us overcome our personal limitations and biases, so that we can formulate a more comprehensive response to God. It helps us supply for our personal lack of initiative in overcoming our deficiencies. It can stir new faith in us, for belief is communicated by believers; and it can stir new love of God in us, for love is communicated by lovers. In brief, the preached retreat is especially valuable in those times when for one reason or another, we need the word of God preached to us through the agency of human beings.

If this information and these norms do not yet make it clear which retreat to prefer, I would offer one piece of advice. Experiment. Try the one you haven't experienced. For St. Ignatius, and for many of us today, the need for experimentation is one of the fundamental principles of the spiritual life.

Chapter Five

Consciousness Examen
by
George A. Aschenbrenner, S.J.

Examen is usually the first practice to disappear from
the daily life of the religious. This occurs for many
reasons; but all the reasons amount to the admission (rarely
explicit) that it is not of immediate practical value in a busy
day. My point in this chapter is that all these reasons and
their false conclusion spring from a basic misunderstand-
ing of the examen as practiced in religious life. Examen
must be seen in relationship to discernment of spirits. It is
a daily intensive exercise of discernment in a person's life.

Examen of Consciousness

For many youth today life is spontaneity if anything. If
spontaneity is crushed or aborted, then life itself is still-
born. In this view examen is living life once removed from
the spontaneity of life. It is a reflective, dehydrated
approach which dries all the spontaneity out of life. These
people today disagree with Socrates' claim that the unex-
amined life is not worth living. For these people the Spirit
is in the spontaneous and so anything that militates against
spontaneity is un-Spirit-ual.

This view overlooks the fact that welling up in the consciousness and experience of each of us are two spontanei-
ties, one good and for God, another evil and not for God.
These two types of spontaneous urges and movements
happen to all of us. So often the quick-witted, loose-

tongued person who can be so entertaining and the center of attention and who is always characterized as being so spontaneous is not certainly being moved by and giving expression to the good spontaneity. For one eager to love God with his or her whole being, the challenge is not simply to let the spontaneous happen but rather to be able to sift out these various spontaneous urges and give full existential ratification to those spontaneous feelings that are from and for God. We do this by allowing the truly Spirited-spontaneity to happen in our daily lives. But we must learn the feel of this true Spirited-spontaneity. Examen has a very central role in this learning.

When examen is related to discernment, it becomes examen of co*nsciousness* rather than of conscience. Examen of conscience has narrow moralistic overtones. Though we were always told that examen of conscience in religious life was not the same as a preparation for confession, it was actually explained and treated as though it were much the same. The prime concern was with what good or bad actions we had done each day. In discernment the prime concern is not with the morality of good or bad actions; rather the concern is how the Lord is affecting and moving us (often quite spontaneously!) deep in our own affective consciousness. What is happening in our consciousness is prior to and more important than our actions which can be delineated as juridically good or evil. How we are experiencing the "drawing" of the Father (Jn 6:44) in our own existential consciousness and how our sinful nature is quietly tempting us and luring us away from our Father in subtle dispositions of our consciousness – this is what the daily examen is concerned with prior to a concern for our response in our *actions*. So it is examen of consciousness that we are concerned with here, so that we can cooperate with and let happen that beautiful spontaneity in our hearts which is the touch of our Father and the urging of the Spirit.

Examen and Religious Identity

The examen we are talking about here is not a Ben Franklin-like striving for self-perfection. We are talking about an experience in faith of growing sensitivity to the unique, intimately special ways that the Lord's spirit has of approaching and calling us. Obviously it takes time for this growth. But in this sense examen is a daily renewal and growth in our religious identity—this unique flesh-spirit person being loved by God and called by Him deep in his personal affective world. It is not possible for me to make an examen without confronting my own identity in Christ before the Father—my own religious identity as poor, celibate, and obedient in imitation of Christ as experienced in the charism of my religious vocation.

And yet so often our daily examen becomes so general and vague and unspecific that our religious identity (Jesuit, Dominican, Franciscan, and so forth) does not seem to make any difference. Examen assumes real value when it becomes a daily experience of confrontation and renewal of our unique religious identity and how the Lord is subtly inviting us to deepen and develop this identity. We should make examen each time with as precise a grasp as we have now on our religious identity. We do not make it just as any Christian but as this specific Christian person with a unique vocation and grace in faith.

Examen and Prayer

The examen is a time of prayer. The dangers of an empty self-reflection or an unhealthy self-centered intro-spection are very real. On the other hand, a lack of effort at examen and the approach of living according to what comes naturally keeps us quite superficial and insensitive to the subtle and profound ways of the Lord deep in our hearts. The prayerful quality and effectiveness of the examen itself depends upon its relationship to the continuing contemplative prayer of the person. Without this relationship examen slips to the level of self-reflection for self-perfection, if it perdures at all.

In daily contemplative prayer the Father reveals to us at His own pace the order of the mystery of all reality in Christ—as Paul says to the Colossians: "... those to whom God has planned to give a vision of the full wonder and splendor of his secret plan for the nations" (Col. 1:27). The contemplator experiences in many subtle, chiefly nonverbal, ways this revelation of the Father in Christ. The presence of the Spirit of the risen Jesus in the heart of the believer makes it possible to sense and "hear" this invitation (challenge!) to order ourselves to this revelation. Contemplation is empty without this "ordering" response.

This kind of reverent, docile (the "obedience of faith" Paul speaks of in Rom. 16:26), and non-moralistic ordering is the work of the daily examen – to sense and recognize those interior invitations of the Lord that guide and deepen this ordering from day to day and not to cooperate with those subtle insinuations opposed to that ordering. Without that contemplative contact with the Father's revelation of reality in Christ, both in formal prayer and informal prayerfulness, the daily practice of examen becomes empty; it shrivels up and dies. Without this "listening" to the Father's revelation of His ways which are so different from our own (Is. 55:8-9), examen again becomes that shaping up of ourselves which is human and natural self-perfection or, even worse, it can become that selfish ordering of ourselves to our own ways.

Examen without regular contemplation is futile. A failure at regular contemplation emaciates the beautifully rich experience of response-ible ordering which the contemplative is continually invited to by the Lord. It is true, on the other hand, that contemplation without regular examen becomes compartmentalized and superficial and stunted in a person's life. The time of formal prayer can become a very sacrosanct period in a person's day but so isolated from the rest of his life that he is not prayerful (finding God in all things) at that level where he really lives. The examen gives our daily contemplative experience of God real bite into all our daily living; it is an important means to finding God in everything and not just in the time of formal prayer, as we will explain at the end of this chapter.

A Discerning Vision of Heart

When we first learned about the examen in religious life, it was a specific exercise of prayer for about a quarter of an hour. And at first it seemed quite stylized and almost artificial. This problem was not in the examen-prayer but in ourselves; we were beginners and had not yet worked out that integration in ourselves of a process of personal discernment to be expressed in daily examens. For the beginner, before he has achieved much of a personalized integration, an exercise or process can be very valuable and yet seem formal and stylized. This should not put us off. It will be the inevitable experience in religious life for the novice and for the "old-timer" who is beginning again at examen.

But examen will fundamentally be misunderstood if the goal of this exercise is not grasped. The specific exercise of examen is ultimately aimed at developing a heart with a discerning vision to be active not only for one or two quarter-hour periods in a day but continually. This is a gift from the Lord—a most important one as Solomon realized (1 Kings 3:9-12). So we must constantly pray for this gift, but we must also be receptive to its development within our hearts. A daily practice of examen is essential to this development.

Hence the five steps of the exercise of examen as presented in the *Spiritual Exercises* of St. Ignatius Loyola (#43) are to be seen, and gradually experienced in faith, as dimensions of the Christian consciousness, formed by God and His work in the heart as it confronts and grows within this world and all of reality. If we allow the Father gradually to transform our mind and heart into that of His Son, to become truly Christian, through our living experience in this world, then the examen, with its separate elements now seen as integrated dimensions of our own consciousness looking out on the world, is much more organic to our outlook and will seem much less contrived. So there is no ideal time allocation for the five elements of the examen each time but rather a daily organic expression of the spiritual mood of the heart. At one time we are drawn to one element longer than the others and at another time to another element over the others.

The mature Ignatius near the end of his life was always examining every movement and inclination of his heart which means he was *discerning* the congruence of everything with his true Christ-centered self. This was the overflow of those regular intensive prayer-exercises of examen every day. The novice or "old-timer" must be aware both of the point of the one or two quarter-hour exercises of examen each day, namely, a continually discerning heart, and of the necessary gradual adaptation of his practice of examen to his stage of development and the situation in the world in which he finds himself. And yet we are all aware of the subtle rationalization of giving up formal examen each day because we have "arrived at" that continually discerning heart. This kind of rationalization will prevent further growth in faith sensitivity to the Spirit and His ways in our daily lives.

Let us now take a look at the format of the examen as presented by St. Ignatius in the *Spiritual Exercises*, #43, but in light of these previous comments on examen as discerning consciousness within the world.

Prayer for Enlightenment

In the *Exercises* Ignatius has an act of thanksgiving as the first part of the examen. The first two parts could be interchanged without too much difference. In fact, I would suggest the prayer for enlightenment as a fitting introduction to the examen.

The examen is not simply a matter of a person's natural power of memory and analysis going back over a part of the day. It is a matter of Spirit-guided insight into my life and courageously responsive sensitivity to God's call in my heart. What we are seeking here is that gradually growing appreciative insight into the mystery which I am. Without the Father's revealing grace this kind of insight is not possible. The Christian must be careful not to get locked into the world of his own human natural powers. Our technological world can pose as a special danger in this regard. Founded on a deep appreciation of the humanly interpersonal, the Christian in faith transcends the boundaries of the here-and-now with its limited natural causality and discovers a Father who loves and works in and through and beyond all. For this reason we begin the examen with an explicit petition for that enlightenment which will occur in and through our own powers but which our own natural powers could never be capable of all by themselves. That the Spirit may help me to see myself a bit more as He sees me Himself!

Reflective Thanksgiving

The stance of a Christian in the midst of the world is that of a poor person, possessing nothing, not even himself, and yet being gifted at every instant in and through everything. When we become too affluently involved with ourselves and deny our inherent poverty, then we lose the gifts and either begin to make demands for what we think we deserve (often leading to angry frustration) or we blandly take for granted *all* that comes our way. Only the truly poor person can appreciate the slightest gift and feel genuine gratitude. The more deeply we live in faith the poorer we are and the more gifted; life itself becomes humble, joyful thanksgiving. This should gradually become an element of our abiding consciousness.

After the introductory prayer for enlightenment our hearts should rest in genuine faith-filled gratitude to our Father for His gifts in this most recent part of the day. Perhaps in the spontaneity of the happening we were not aware of the gift and now in this exercise of reflective prayer we see the events in a very different perspective. Our sudden gratitude—now the act of a humble selfless pauper—helps make us ready to discover the gift more clearly in a future sudden spontaneity. Our gratitude should center on the concrete, uniquely personal gifts that each of us was blessed with, whether large and obviously important or tiny and apparently insignificant. There is much in our lives that we take for granted; gradually He will lead us to a deep realization that *all is gift.* It is right to give Him praise and thanks!

Practical Survey of Actions

In this third element of the examen ordinarily we rush to review, in some specific detail, our actions of that part of the day just finished so we can catalogue them as good or bad. Just what we shouldn't do! Our prime concern here in faith is what has been happening to us and in us since the last examen. The operative questions are: What has been happening in us, how has the Lord been working in us, what has He been asking us? And only secondarily are our own actions to be considered. This part of the examen presumes that we have become sensitive to our interior feelings, moods, and slightest urgings and that we are not frightened by them but have learned to take them very seriously. It is here in the depths of our affectivity, so spontaneous, strong, and shadowy at times, that God moves us and deals with us most intimately. These interior moods, feelings, urges, and movements are the "spirits" that must be sifted out, discerned, so we can recognize the Lord's call to us at this intimate core of our being. As we have said above, the examen is a chief means to this discerning of our interior consciousness.

This presumes a real faith approach to life – that life is first listening, then acting in response:

> The fundamental attitude of the believer is of one who listens. It is to the Lord's utterances that he gives ear. In as many different ways and on as many varied levels as the listener can discern the word and will of the Lord manifested to him, he must respond with all the Pauline "obedience of faith." . . . It is the attitude of receptivity, passivity and poverty of one who is always in need, radically dependent, conscious of his creature-hood.[1]

Hence the great need for interior quiet, peace, and a passionate receptivity that attunes us to listening to God's word at every instant and in every situation and *then* responding in our own activity. Again in a world that is founded more on activity (becoming activism), productivity, and efficiency (whereas efficacity is a norm for the kingdom of God!) this faith view is implicitly, if not explicitly, challenged at every turn in the road.

And so our first concern here is with these subtle intimate, affective ways in which the Lord has been dealing with us during these past few hours. Perhaps we did not recognize Him calling in that past moment, but now our vision is clear and direct. Secondarily our concern is with our actions insofar as they were *responses* to His calling. So often our activity becomes primary to us and all sense of response in our activity is lost. We become self-moved and motivated rather than moved and motivated by the Spirit (Rom 8:14). This is a subtle lack of faith and failure to live as a son or daughter of our Father. In the light of faith it is the *quality* (of responsive-ness) of the activity, more than the activity itself, which makes the difference for the kingdom of God.

In this general review there is no strain to reproduce every second since the last examen; rather our concern is with specific details and incidents as they reveal patterns and bring some clarity and insight. This brings us to a consideration of what Ignatius calls the particular examen.

This element of the examen, perhaps more than any other, has been misunderstood. It has often become an effort to divide and conquer by moving down the list of vices or up the list of virtues in a mechanically planned approach to self-perfection. A certain amount of time was spent on each vice or virtue one by one, and then we moved on to the next one on the list. Rather than a practical programmed approach to perfection, the particular examen is meant to be a reverently honest, personal meeting with the Lord in our own hearts.

When we become sensitive and serious enough about loving God, we begin to realize some changes must be made. We are deficient in so many areas and so many defects must be done away with. But the Lord does not want all of them to be handled at once. Usually there is one area of our hearts where He is especially calling for conversion which is always the beginning of new life. He is interiorly nudging us in one area and reminding us that if we are really serious about Him this one aspect of ourselves must be changed. This is often precisely the one area we want to forget and (maybe!) work on later. We do not want to let His word condemn us in this one area and so we try to forget it and distract ourselves by working on some other safer area which *does* require conversion but not with the same urgent sting of consciousness that is true of the former area. It is in this first area of our hearts, if we will be honest and open with the Lord, where we are very personally experiencing the Lord in the burning fire of His Word as He confronts us here and now. So often we fail to recognize this guilt for what it really is or we try to blunt it by working hard on something else that *we* may want to correct whereas the Lord wants something else here and now. For beginners it takes time to become interiorly sensitive to God before they gradually come to recognize the Lord's call to conversion (maybe involving a very painful struggle!) in some area of their lives. It is better for beginners to take this time to learn what the Lord wants their particular examen now to be rather than just taking some assigned imperfection to get started on.

And so the particular examen is very personal, honest, and at times a very subtle experience of the Lord calling in our hearts for deeper conversion to Himself. The matter of the conversion may remain the same for a long period of time, but the important thing is our sense of His personal challenge to us. Often this experience of the Lord calling for conversion in one small part of our hearts takes the expression of good healthy guilt which should be carefully interpreted and responded to if there is to be progress in holiness. When the particular examen is seen as this personal experience of the Lord's love for us, then we can understand why St. Ignatius suggests that we turn our whole consciousness to this experience of the Lord (whatever it be in all practicality, for example, more subtle humility or readiness to get involved with people on their terms, etc.) at those two very important moments in our day, when we begin our day and when we close it, besides the formal examen times.

In this third dimension of the formal examen the growing faith sense of our sinfulness is very central. This is more of a spiritual faith reality as revealed by the Father in our experience than a heavily moralistic and guilt-laden reality. A deep sense of sinfulness depends on our growth in faith and is a dynamic realization which always ends in thanksgiving—the song of the "saved sinner." In his book *Growth in the Spirit*, François Roustang, in the second chapter, speaks very profoundly about sinfulness and thanksgiving. This can provide enormous insight into the relationship of these second and third elements of the formal examen, especially as dimensions of our abiding Christian consciousness.

Contrition and Sorrow

The Christian heart is always a heart in song—a song of deep joy and gratitude. But the Alleluia can be quite superficial and without body and depth unless it is genuinely touched with sorrow. This is the song of a sinner constantly aware of being prey to his sinful tendencies and yet being converted into the newness which is guaranteed in the victory of Jesus Christ. Hence, we never grow out of a sense of wonder-ful sorrow in the presence of our Savior.

This basic dimension of our heart's vision which the Father desires to deepen in us as He converts us from sinners to His sons and daughters, if we allow Him, is here applied to the specifics of our actions since the last examen, especially insofar as they were selfishly inadequate *responses* to the Lord's work in our hearts. This sorrow will especially spring from the lack of honesty and courage in responding to the Lord's call in the particular examen. This contrition and sorrow is not a shame nor a depression at our weakness but a faith experience as we grow in our realization of our Father's awesome desire that we love Him with every ounce of our being.

After this description, the value of pausing each day in formal examen and giving concrete expression to this abiding sense of sorrow in our hearts should be quite obvious and should flow naturally from the third element of practical survey of our actions.

Hopeful Resolution for Future

This final element of the formal daily examen grows very naturally out of the previous elements. The organic development leads us to face the future which is now rising to encounter us and become integrated into our lives. In the light of our present discernment of the immediate past how do we look to the future? Are we discouraged or despondent or fearful of the future? If this is the atmosphere of our hearts now, we must wonder why and try to interpret this atmosphere; we must be honest in acknowledging our feeling for the future, and not repress it by hoping it will go away.

The precise expression of this final element will be determined by the organic flow of this precise examen now. Accordingly, this element of resolution for the immediate future will never happen the same way each time. If it did happen in the same expression each time, it would be a sure sign that we were not really entering into the previous four elements of the examen.

At this point in the examen there should be a great desire to face the future with renewed vision and sensitivity as we pray both to recognize even more the subtle ways in which the Lord will greet us and to hear His Word call us in the existential situation of the future and to respond to His call with more faith, humility, and courage. This should be especially true of that intimate abiding experience of the Lord calling for painful conversion in some area of our heart—what we have called the particular examen. A great hope should be the atmosphere of our hearts at this point—a hope not founded on our own deserts, or our own powers for the future, but rather founded much more fully in our Father whose glorious victory in Jesus Christ we share through the life of Their Spirit in our hearts. The more we will trust God and allow Him to lead in our lives, the more we will experience true supernatural hope in God painfully in and through, but quite beyond, our own weak powers—an experience at times frightening and emptying but ultimately joyfully exhilarating. St. Paul in this whole passage from the Letter to the Philippians (3:7-14) expresses well the spirit of this conclusion of the formal examen: ". . . I leave the past behind and with hands outstretched to whatever lies ahead I go straight for the goal" (3:13).

Examen and Discernment

We will close this chapter with some summary remarks about the examen, as here described, and discernment of spirits. When examen is understood in this light and so practiced each day, then it becomes so much more than just a brief exercise performed once or twice a day and which is quite secondary to our formal prayer and active living of God's love in our daily situation. Rather it becomes an exercise which so focuses and renews our specific faith identity that we should be even more reluctant to omit our examen than our formal contemplative prayer each day. This seems to have been St. Ignatius' view of the practice of the examen. He never talks of omitting it though he does talk of adapting and abbreviating the daily meditation for various reasons. For him it seems the examen was central and quite inviolate. This strikes us as strange until we revamp our understanding of the examen. Then perhaps we begin to see the examen as so intimately connected to our growing identity and so important to our finding God in all things at all times that it becomes our central daily experience of prayer.

For Ignatius finding God in all things is what life is all about. Near the end of his life he said that "whenever he wished, at whatever hour, he could find God" (*Autobiography*, #99). This is the mature Ignatius who had so fully allowed God to possess every ounce of his being through a clear YES to the Father that radiated from the very core of his being, that he could be conscious at any moment he wanted of the deep peace, joy, and contentment (consolation, see the *Exercises*, #316) which was the experience of God at the center of his heart. Ignatius' identity, at this point in his life, was quite fully and clearly "in Christ" as Paul says: "For now my place is in him, and I am not dependent upon any of the self-achieved righteousness of the Law" (Phil. 3:9); Ignatius knew and was his true self in Christ.

Being able to find God whenever he wanted, Ignatius was now able to find Him in all things through a test for congruence of any interior impulse, mood, or feeling with his true self. Whenever he found interior consonance within himself (which registers as peace, joy, contentment again) from the immediate interior movement and felt himself being his true congruent self, then he knew he had heard God's word to him at that instant. And he responded with that fullness of humble courage so typical of Ignatius. If he discovered interior dissonance, agitation, and disturbance "at the bottom of the heart" (to be carefully distinguished from repugnance "at the top of the head"[2]) and could not find his true congruent self in Christ, then he recognized the interior impulse as an "evil spirit" and he experienced God by "going against" the desolate impulse (cf. *Exercises*, #319). In this way he was able to find God in all things by carefully discerning all his interior experiences ("spirits"). Thus discernment of spirits became a daily very practical living of the art of loving God with his whole heart, whole body, and whole strength. Every moment of life was loving (finding) God in the existential situation in a deep quiet, peace, and joy.

For Ignatius, this finding God in the present interior movement, feeling, or option was almost instantaneous in his mature years because the central "feel" or "bent" of his being had so been grasped by God. For the beginner, what was almost instantaneous for the mature Ignatius may require the effort of a prayerful process of a few hours or days depending on the importance of the movement-impulse to be discerned. In some of his writings, Ignatius uses examen to refer to this almost instantaneous test for congruence with his true self—something he could do a number of times every hour of the day. But he also speaks of examen in the formal restricted sense of two quarter-hour exercises of prayer a day.

The intimate and essential relationship between these two senses of examen has been the point of this whole chapter.

Notes

[1] David Asselin, S.J., "Christian Maturity and Spiritual Discernment," *Review for Religious,* v. 27 (1968), p. 594.

[2] John Carroll Futrell, S.J., *Ignatian Discernment* (St. Louis: Institute of Jesuit Sources, 1970), p. 64.